SPORT COMPACTS

Alan Paradise

MBI

This edition first published in 2003 by Motorbooks International, an imprint of MBI Publishing Company, Galtier Plaza, Suite 200, 380 Jackson Street, St. Paul, MN 55101-3885 USA

The information in this book is true and complete to the best of our knowledge. All recommendations are made without any guarantee on the part of the author or Publisher, who also disclaim any liability incurred in connection with the use of this data or specific details.

We recognize that some words, model names and designations, for example, mentioned herein are the property of the trademark holder. We use them for identification purposes only. This is not an official publication.

Motorbooks International titles are also available at discounts in bulk quantity for industrial or sales-promotional use. For details write to Special Sales Manager at Motorbooks International Wholesalers & Distributors, Galtier Plaza, Suite 200, 380 Jackson Street, St. Paul, MN 55101-3885 USA.

Library of Congress Cataloging-in-Publication Data

Paradise, Alan.
    Sport compacts / by Alan Paradise.
        p. cm.
    ISBN 0-7603-1496-9 (pbk. : alk. paper)
        1. Sports cars. 2. Compact cars. I. Title.

TL236.P25 2003
629.222'1—dc21

On the front cover: *Bottom right:* This is an example of the worldwide reach of the sport compact movement, as a tricked-out Dodge Neon lines up alongside a slick pair of Honda Civics with a Ford Focus in the distance. *Left:* A group of hot sport compacts take to the track at California Speedway. *Center Right:* Two of the hottest roadsters around are the Honda S2000 and Mazda's Miata. *Title page:* Dave Rifkin built the ultimate California Passat using key components from leading aftermarket companies. The overall effect was a sedan that combined auto electronics, turbo power, and creature upgrades, while retaining a clean European appearance.

On the frontis: A dead giveaway that a turbocharged monster is breathing down your tailpipe is the grinning innercooler mounted front and center.

On the back cover: *Top right:* Lightweight components, such as on this Civic, can serve a dual purpose – they shed weight and provide good ol' fashioned fresh air to the engine. *Bottom left:* Before the WRX, Subaru earned entry into the sport compact community with the Impreza 2.5RS, which at least carried the looks of Subaru's works rally cars, if not the turbocharged horsepower. *Bottom right:* Unlimited performance potential has made the RX-7 a popular sport compact. On the track or at the strip, RX-7s have the ability to strike fear in the hearts of competitors.

Edited by Peter Bodensteiner
Designed by Brenda Canales

Printed in China

TABLE OF CONTENTS

FOREWORD & ACKNOWLEDGMENTS

Automotive performance and customizing is, by its nature, an individualistic venture. For some it's all about speed. Others are into the glitz and glamour.

Not since the 1960s, an era many old-school car guys refer to as the golden age of speed and beauty, has there been a more fired-up gaggle of enthusiasts than those who make up the sport compact car world.

Bringing the interest of sport compacting to the forefront has taken the vision and efforts of many people – most of whom have never been given a mention or credit for their contributions. I will remedy that situation right here and now. Larry Saavedra took over for me as the editor of *Sport Compact Car* magazine in 1994 and carefully guided it for six years.

Matt Pearson, formerly of *Super Street* magazine, and now with Honda, has been another editorial influence that formed the past and helped shape the future. Let us not forget Howard Lim (*Super Street* publisher) and John Dianna (head buckaroo of HCI) for their efforts to bring new voices to print. Of course, none of the leading publications would exist without the courage of the late Ken Yee. As the decisionmaker at McMullen-Yee Publishing, he gave me the go-ahead to create *Sport Compact Car* magazine and dedicated the funding to get it off the ground.

On the product side of the ledger, we all know Oscar Jackson to be one of the more innovative and knowledgeable people to ever fire up a four-cylinder engine. What is not usually brought out is what a truly genuine person he is – always ready to talk performance with anyone and everyone who will listen.

Other behind-the-scenes people who have made invaluable contributions in product development and marketing include Kirk Miller and John Concialdi (AEM), Gary Peek (Eibach Springs), Ron Johnson (Nissan), Tom Matano (Mazda), Tom Scarpello (Ford SVT), Steve Millen (Stillen), and Greg Woo (Neuspeed).

Events have continued to evolve into world-class attractions, mostly due to the tireless efforts of people like Craig Lieberman (former NIRA director), Mike DeFord (Carlisle Events), Michael Meyers (NOPI), and the entire crew at Vision Entertainment.

To make anything happen it takes teamwork or at the very least a group of people dedicated to a common goal. The same holds true with the creation of this book. While my name appears on the cover, a number of talented professionals have helped make *Sport Compacts* possible. For their efforts I would like to acknowledge the following people: Joy Keller, Justin Fort, Wiley Davis, David Rifken, Nicole Leap, Aaron Smith, Nancy Wade, and Mario Caner and the crew at DVimaging.com. Most of all, loving thanks to my wife Annette and son Cory. Their unconditional support is the fuel that drives the engine of my creativity and discipline.

Audiobahn HoseTechniques.com

They seem to have come from nowhere—taking over the streets in a fast and furious fashion. Small, nimble, and aggressive coupes, sedans, and roadsters, locked and loaded with major league attitude. With high-revving, small-bore engines and slammed-to-the-pavement suspensions, the new wave of horsepower known as sport compact cars has forged a place in automotive history.

Laying claim to the concrete and asphalt that once was the domain of '32 highboys and Hemi 'Cudas, sport compact owners offer a new way of thinking to the longstanding tradition of automotive self-expression. The old guard of monster V-8s hasn't completely disappeared; it has just been pushed aside by the drivers of this new performance enthusiast generation. The land of emblems shaped like ovals, bow ties, and pentastars is now overtaken by sleek, hip, chrome-plated logos belonging primarily to Asian automakers. Welcome to the brave new world of sport compact performance.

Before looking at the present and predicting the future of this newest of all automotive interests, it is important to understand the foundation on which sport compacting was built. True small car performance started showing up

Sport compact cars have come from humble beginnings to become an automotive segment that is only rivaled by street rods in terms of size and market share. Unlike other forms of performance and customizing, sport compact makes and models are not dominated by domestic names, but are a combination of brands from around the world. This makes sport compacts a truly global interest.

The roots of small car performance can be traced back to British and German compacts. The Mini Cooper offered excellent power-to-weight performance and the fully independent suspension gave the car handling that rarely required the driver to apply the brakes prior to cornering.

after World War II. New and innovative makes and models began pouring out of war-torn European countries, such as Britain and Germany. A booming American economy became familiar with strange names like Porsche, Triumph, and MG. Along with Lotus, Jaguar, Austin-Healey, and a few Italian upstarts like Fiat, Alfa, and Ferrari, these sports cars were being embraced by a microscopic portion of the United States population. As infectious as these cars were, the interest was not even a blip on the automotive radar screen.

The actual beginning of small car performance at a truly affordable price came from a very unlikely automaker. It had no idea its small, fuel sipping "people's car" would be the start of a groundswell of popularity, a groundswell that would forever change the face of the auto industry. When Volkswagen first came to America, consumers laughed at its odd, rounded shape. At the time we were firmly believed the marketing slogan that bigger was better. However, it didn't take long for the visionaries of performance to discover the potential hidden in the air-cooled VW engine.

Soon after wheel-standing Bugs were shutting down small-block Chevy and Ford V-8-powered door slammers at local drag strips, another European carmaker made its mark in America. BMW released the 2002, a small, nimble, and surprisingly quick coupe that featured a very sophisticated suspension and a build quality not yet imagined by Detroit's automotive brain trust.

While this was happening in the center ring of the automotive circus, outside the spotlight the real future of America's car market was taking shape. The first Toyota dealership opened in 1959 in San Diego, California. When Rose Imports rolled a tiny, boxy, commuter car into its showroom, no one noticed. The buzz in the import world was about the VW. Soon after Toyota arrived, Nissan did as well (under the name of Datsun). Honda, Mazda, and Mitsubishi would follow in subsequent decades. However, throughout the 1960s Toyota and Datsun worked hard to develop a small, loyal audience in the land of twenty-five-cents-per-gallon gasoline.

While both Japanese auto companies were selling cars and trucks, the egos of GM, Ford, Chrysler, and American Motors would lay the seed for sport compacts. In 1967 the four American automakers were in an all-out battle for horsepower supremacy. Bigger and bigger engines with multiple carburetors and escalating power ratings were being marketed as if there was no end to the supply of cheap gasoline. The Sports Car Club of America (SCCA) developed a racing series aimed at pitting a new brand of coupes, nicknamed "Pony Cars," in a series of road races. The Trans-Am series was born, and all four manufacturers quickly jumped headfirst into the game. Mustangs, Falcons, Comets, Cougars, Camaros, Firebirds, and Barracudas were the first models in the hunt for bragging rights and increased Monday-morning sales. Soon new models such as the Javelin and the Challenger emerged. Big-name drivers such as Gurney,

For many, their first taste of compact performance and/or customizing came in the form of a Volkswagen Bug or Beetle. While never intended to be a cult car, Volkswagen enthusiasts quickly discovered its potential.

Donahue, Jones, Foyt, Titus, and others were battling in specially prepared door slammers. It was a great time for auto racing.

During this time SCCA saw an opportunity to create a lower class within Trans-Am racing, one that would allow BMW and Alfa Romeo to bang fenders with the Chevrolet Corvair and the Opel Kadett. It was here that Peter Brock saw the opportunity to run a car he believed would blow the doors off the dominant BMWs. That car was the Datsun 510. With backing from Datsun, Brock put together a car that instantly ran headlight-to-headlight with the BMWs. The masterful part of the plan was that parts departments of Datsun dealers offered many of the same performance parts used on Brock's race cars as over-the-counter items. This made the 510 the first true sport compact car.

Toyota was far behind this way of thinking. Its Corolla and Corona models were not considered in the same performance league as Datsun. Upstart Mazda was getting into the performance market with its rotary-powered coupe. And although Toyota was losing the ego battle, it was winning the sales war with the other Japanese imports, which now included the first Honda model.

During Honda's first decade selling cars on American soil, sales languished far behind Datsun, Toyota, and Mazda. However, the power of its product was the quiet innovation and remarkable European-like quality built into the early CVCC models.

The true turning point in import car sales came from a different kind of import—Saudi oil. The energy crisis that began in 1973 quickly

The first Honda automobile to be imported to the U.S. was this tiny 600. Powered by a 600cc engine producing only 52 horsepower, the 1969 model was underpowered and undersized in a world of big V-8s.

In 1975 Honda introduced the CVCC. This was the first Honda model to enjoy success on the street and at the track.

changed consumer alliance from American land yachts to fuel-efficient Japanese coupes, sedans, wagons, and trucks. Japanese cars and trucks sold as quickly as they could be unloaded from the cargo ships.

Ford and General Motors made the quickest adjustments by releasing rivals to the imports with the Ford Pinto/Mercury Bobcat and the Chevy Vega. Thus the race to offer sporty, afford-able compacts went into high gear.

Small car performance became a sub-culture throughout the late 1970s and early 1980s. The first celebrity personality among import lovers was Oscar Jackson. Jackson was tuning Honda CVCC coupes that were capable of embarrassing Corvettes, Mustangs, and Camaros. From his southern California shop, Jackson created giant killers. Unlike the Volkswagen Bugs that came before, these Hondas could accelerate and corner on an equal or higher level than more presti-gious makes and models. The exacting and diligent efforts of Jackson Racing helped forge the new frontier for Honda and all small car performance enthusiasts.

As the nation recovered from escalating gasoline prices, government emission regula-tions all but strangled the world's automakers' ability to create and market high-performance vehicles. Oddly enough, it was the mass popularity of mini-trucks during the late 1980s and early 1990s that created a marketplace for small car accessories. After the launch of *Sport Compact Car* magazine in December 1989, the interest in performance, handling, electronics, and cosmetic enhancements for small cars grew at a mind-boggling rate.

With its own regular publication and racing events – most notably the early Battle of the

SCCA continued to feature compact performance cars after Trans-Am. Here Stu Fisher drives his 1977 RX-3 to a B Sedan Championship. *Mazda*

Import drag races—the sport compact movement grew and evolved into a performance-based interest. While the mini-truck crowd was showing off ground-scraping ride heights and 1,000+ watt audio systems, sport compact owners were busy fitting turbochargers and coil-over suspensions. The two interests shared many of the same brand names but were clearly headed in opposite directions.

Like many automotive trends, southern California was the eye of the sport compact hurricane. The closely related mini-truck movement began in Los Angeles, Orange, Riverside, San Diego, and Kern counties and spread across the West, infecting Nevada, Arizona, and Texas before moving south into Georgia and Florida. To the surprise of many, sport compact interest didn't move eastward in a wave, but quickly sprouted across the country and in Canada. While California remained the number one state in terms of sheer numbers, New York, the Carolinas, Maryland, Oregon, Washington, Illinois, Tennessee, and Alabama were strong states as early as 1992.

Throughout the 1990s the passion grew at a nearly unprecedented rate. Not since the dawn of hot rodding had a performance automotive interest so captivated a generation. The die had been cast; sport compact cars were not to be a passing fancy, but would establish deep roots and change the way big automakers planned future products and developed marketing plans and advertising campaigns.

The only question left to answer is how this type of automotive personalizing/customizing came to be known as sport compacts. It was a hot, smoggy August day in 1988. Over a Double Double, fries, and a shake at an In-N-Out Burger in Anaheim, California, Steve Stillwell and I were discussing future issues of *Truckin'* and *MiniTruckin'*, the magazines we worked on together, he as editor and I as the feature editor. We commented on the rapid growth of tricked-out compact cars that had become part of the area's mini-truck scene. I remarked that I believed this could be the next big enthusiast market. He agreed and I set out on an eight-month stealth mission to develop a new publication aimed at a yet-to-be-named group.

When sufficient materials had been gathered to create a minimum of two issues, Steve and I met with McMullen Publishing VP Ken Yee. As we viewed what would prove to be the foundation for the firm's future halo title, names were bantered about. The one that stuck was *Sport Compact Car*. The definition for this new niche was created. From that point on there has been no looking back.

While the public saw compact cars as economical and nimble, sport compacters realized the drag racing possibilities of the cars and quickly established a new sport: Import drag racing. *Matt Pearson*

CHAPTER 2

By 1987 the foundation for sport compacting was beginning to take shape. At the forefront of the movement were three automakers: Nissan, Ford, and Honda. In the Nissan camp was the Sentra, with its BMW-like styling. Ford dealers were parading the Escort as its small car answer to the more expensive Mustang. Honda had the Civic and CRX. As an automaker, however, it paid little attention to enthusiasts' interests.

Nissan was slightly ahead of the market with its factory race program that included street-legal components for the production-based Sentra. Ford's Escort benefited from its European styling and offered an above-average starting point with the GT model option. Without really trying, Honda unknowingly sold Civic and CRX models to enthusiasts, due in large part to the fact that Jackson Racing had proven the cars could go fast on Sunday and make it to work (or school) on Monday. From these three makes and four models, the foundation for the sport took hold and immediately accelerated to warp speed.

By 1990 the rapidly growing sport compact world expanded to consider new models. By

Muscle car wars are primarily made up of Chrysler, GM, and Ford models. In the sport compact car world the selections extend far beyond the Big Three. Aside from the domestic brands, the majority of enthusiasts look to the East for inspiration. This is an example of the worldwide reach of the sport, as a tricked-out Dodge Neon lines up alongside a slick pair of Honda Civics with a Ford Focus in the distance.

Popularity for Datsun's 510 spilled over from the track to the street. Both coupe and sedan models remain desirable street cars, aided by plenty of support from the aftermarket and from Nissan.

now the entire Honda line (Civic, CRX, Accord, and Prelude) were primary targets. Toyota started to get into the game with the Celica and MR2. Nissan stepped up to add the 240SX, NX, and Maxima. Mazda made big news with Miata, Protégé, and MX3 models. On the domestic front, Ford brought on the Probe. Chevy, desperate for any form of market share, tried the Cavalier brand. However, the popularity for any and all of these models hinged on the willingness of the automotive aftermarket to respond with performance and cosmetic products.

Honda emerged as the clear winner. Mazda rallied around the Miata, a car that should have made major inroads in the hearts and minds of sport compacters. However, the greed of dealers soon after its release sealed the

Far and away the leading make and model in the sport compact car world is the Civic. This is a classic example of the quintessential Civic street machine –featuring a hammered suspension, trick Ts & Ws, big wing, styling package, free-flowing exhaust, air intake, and race-inspired interior trim.

Either for show or go, the Civic has been the mainstay of the sport compact car scene. This sedan sports wild graphics and shaved trim to grab attention on the street or at shows.

Miata's fate, as potential buyers proved to be older and far outside the mainstream demographic of sport compacting.

The segment has since grown to include models like the Nissan 300ZX, Toyota Supra, Mazda RX-7, and Acura NSX, as each have become affordable as preowned cars.

Many of the key cars that have made sport compacting what it is today no longer exist in current model product lines. Nameplates like Integra, Escort, Probe, Contour, Storm, CRX, del Sol, Supra, and RX-7 have all been retired from the American market. However many models, especially the Integra, CRX, Supra, and RX-7, enjoy a lasting and loyal following, making each a player in the ongoing street and track scene.

Civic Pride

The undisputed champion and poster child for sport compact cars is the Honda Civic. As Oscar Jackson said in 1998, "The Civic is this generation's 1955 Chevy." In the entire sport

Honda released the hot 170hp Si in 1999. This gave Honda a much-needed image boost at a time when For, Mitsubishi and Toyota were beginning to take up the slack and challenge the Japanese carmaker for street supremacy.

Honda followed up the 99 Si with a new, sweeter model in 2002. The later version featured improved acceleration mainly due to a better power-to-weight ratio and revised gearing. *DVimaging*

The one downfall of the Civic is the performance limits of its SOHV engine. Even in early VTEC form there was (and still is) only a finite amount of horsepower that could be reliably squeezed from the 1.6 liter SOHC format. When Honda reintroduced the Si in 1999, the DOHV VTEC engine was standard, and it set Civic lovers on a search-and-destroy mission for all those Mitsubishi Eclipse owners who had embarrassed them prior to the new Si release.

As time marches on, the Si remains the gold standard for Civic enthusiasts. While the newer shape is not as attractive, the car's performance and refinement have improved each year.

Civic enthusiasts are fiercely loyal to the model. Few owners' groups can mount a challenge to the passion Civic owners feel for their cars. The car's visual versatility and balanced performance, coupled with its ease of modification, has made the Civic the ideal entry-level vehicle into the sport compact car world.

compact arena, there are more performance and customizing parts available for the Civic than for any other compact sedan, coupe, or two-seater. The only serious challenger to the Civic in this category is the Miata.

The Civic is a passive, practical car by nature—much the same as its German inspiration, the Volkswagen Beetle. However, with an entire array of performance parts tempting every Civic owner, it's not hard to see why this is the most upgraded car on the planet.

Honda's Civic features a platform that begs to be upgraded. During the early 1990s Civic owners took boxy hatchbacks, particularly the better-performing Si models, and turned them into stylish street machines. Using key components from the aftermarket, Civics could easily be transformed from bland grocery getters to weekend warriors. Nearly any Civic could be made into a respectable performer, or just personalized to look like one.

Integra & RSX, the Next Steps

The natural progression for a large number of Civic owners is the step up to the Acura Integra. Until 2001 Integra was the upscale Civic, as far as Honda/Acura fans were concerned. In 2001 the Integra name was dropped from the Acura line and replaced with a new showroom silhouette called the RSX. While the new model quickly proved it could be a qualified successor to the Integra, many Honda Civic owners felt betrayed by the change in factory direction. This turned up the heat in the pre-owned Integra market.

Like Civic models, Integras are available in various trim and performance levels. There are VTEC and non-VTEC engines, two-and four-door models, and even an early hatchback. However, hands down, the most desirable, sought-after and admired version is the Type R. Acura created a true factory hot rod in the Type R. The tuned 1.8 liter VTEC engine pumps out over 190 horsepower without the assistance of forced induction. The suspension features more aggressive shock damping, increased spring stiffness, and thicker anti-roll bars. The shifter

It didn't take long for modified versions of the RSX (the Integra replacement) to show up. This factory-tuner version demonstrates how the vision and attitude at Honda/Acura has changed over the past few years. *Honda*

provides short, sweet throws, and the exhaust is tuned to deliver improved performance and torque on both the low and top end. This is all before bolting on a single aftermarket product.

The Type R is the high-end model and is very rare. Fewer than 10,000 were produced over a three-year period. The GS-R is the most accessible performance version and can be

Without the Civic, Acura's Integra would be the most popular kid on the sport compact block. Serving as the logical upgrade from the entry-level Honda, the Integra features excellent overall performance with unquestionable quality and durability. It is also a sure bet for aftermarket manufacturers, making it a car that can be modified or personalized with infinite possibilities.

The Integra platform and drivetrain make it an ideal choice for all forms of motorsports, especially drag racing. *DVimaging*

Accord offers additional size and power, but at the cost of overall performance. For many, the trade-off is worth the added style and creature comforts.

quite a kick to drive. By simply adding a few key aftermarket components, such as a cold-air intake, high-flow catalytic converter, tuned exhaust, and a set of performance tires, wheels and springs, the GS-R model is an instant object of envy.

> ### ▼ THE ONES
>
> **1988:** First year Honda/Acura got it right. Good array of performance parts available.
> **1992 GS-R:** Zero to 60 in under seven seconds–what more need be said?
> **1994-98 GS-R:** New 1.8 liter engine with 170 horsepower in a sporty shell.
> **2002 RSX:** Change of name and change in attitude.

All the King's Horses

It has been well established that Honda's Civic sits on the sport compact throne and Acura's Integra sits just to the left of center court. But there are other Hondas that share in the glory of being in the royal sport compact family.

Placed directly behind the Civic and Integra for supremacy is the Honda Accord, followed by the Prelude. Both of these bigger Hondas share components and provide unique advantages to enthusiasts willing to pony up the extra dollars needed to own and trick out these models.

The Accords have long been the backbone of Honda's general consumer sales. For more than a decade the Accord has run headlight-to-headlight with Toyota's Camry and Ford's Taurus as the best-selling car in America. The Camry and Taurus do not appear on the sport compact radar screen, but the Accord is and has always been a major blip.

The reason for the Accord's success with sport compacters is easy to understand. In either two- or four-door versions the model offers enthusiasts so many options it's tough to dispute its versatility and potential. Go fast, look good, handle well, and ride in luxury; it's all possible–and can be done at the same time.

The semi-sports car brother to the Accord is the Prelude. Many Honda fans considered the Prelude to be the ultimate dream machine, until Honda introduced the S2000 in October 1999.

Honda has always doted on the Prelude. When it was first released in 1977 it propelled the Honda name into uncharted waters. Despite underwhelming engine performance, the styling won the hearts of consumers – especially females. As the Honda line matured so did the Prelude's sophistication, refinement, and overall performance.

The true sports-coupe of Honda has always been the Prelude. This version features all the trick bells and whistles including a fully worked suspension, 19-inch Ts & Ws, leather interior, bolt-on engine performance tricks, and a styling package that accentuates the Honda body lines.

▼ THE ONES

1977 Accord: Second year of production worked out the bugs. Clean styling and shared performance items with CVCC.

1983 Prelude: Plenty of elements available to make a low-buck racer. Antiquated but cool shape.

1987 Accord: Fuel injection now standard, aerodynamic styling, much improved transmission and suspension.

1987 Prelude: More power, comfort, and better suspension.

1990 Prelude Si: Four-wheel steering option, 125 horsepower and the final year of generation three shape.

1991 Accord SE: More ponies (2.2 liter 140 horsepower), four-wheel disc brakes, leather seats.

1995 Accord EX: First year of the 2.2 liter VTEC.

1995 Prelude: Low production numbers, good power, good value.

1998 Prelude: Good power-to-weight and improved torque, sweet styling, excellent handling.

2000 Accord EX: Powerful 200 horsepower V-6, more style, and performance parts to spare.

Today the Prelude is viewed as a world-class performance sports coupe. Because it's a Honda, it has all the power, suspension, and cosmetic items necessary to create a personal performance statement.

The Diamond Star Coalition

Over the past decade Mitsubishi has emerged as a more serious player – primarily on the wings of two models, the Eclipse and, more recently, the Lancer. However, it wasn't always that way. Many Mitsubishi-made cars have floated in and out of the sport compact scene – most are better identified with other names, such as Dodge, Plymouth, and Eagle. These cars were easily on the edge of the sport compact car envelope. Mitsubishi power became much better known with the launch of the Eclipse and the domestic brand derivative Eagle Talon. With this, it only took a few years for Mitsubishi to become a common garage name in the niche's vernacular.

Mitsubishi has developed a loyal following mainly on the merits of the Eclipse. Seen as a viable alternative to anything Honda, Eclipses of all generations are popular in all forms of grassroots sport compact motorsports. *DVimaging*

In stunning yellow, this Spyder model shows the traffic- stopping potential of the Eclipse's third generation styling. So impressive was this creation that Mitsubishi displayed it as part of its International Autoshow display.

For 10 years the Eclipse, with its powerful turbocharged four-cylinder engine and optional all-wheel-drive, captured the hearts of sport compact enthusiasts. Certainly, these cars continue to provide tremendous bang-for-the-buck on the used market. The third generation Eclipse struck a chord with a slightly different breed of enthusiast and quickly became a popular platform to build upon. Gen-three Eclipse models can be found in either four- or six-cylinder models. The bigger, more powerful V-6s enjoy a better power-to-weight ratio, but suffer from a lack of off-the-shelf performance parts. On the other hand, the four-cylinder versions can be made to perform at a very respectable level without the need for internal engine modifications. While the Spyder established the sexy part of the line, the coupe clearly is the popular choice, and with good reason. The structural rigidity of an attached roof greatly enhances the car's handling capabilities. The unusually soft factory suspension is a weak point of the Eclipse, but it is nothing that can't easily be upgraded using aftermarket components.

The big things that Eclipse models have always delivered are massive proportions of style and image. Mitsubishi can never be accused of leaving modeling clay on the studio floor when it comes to its halo model. Each progression of the Eclipse has proven to boost Mitsubishi sales as well as the carmaker's image.

The sales and enthusiast success of the Eclipse led to the 2002 introduction of the Lancer. The first edition to hit American roads was a severely watered-down version of the highly successful European rally racer. However, it was the right car for many who longed for a Japanese alternative to the Civic. The downside was that it had to compete in the "other than Honda" class with a newly designed Nissan Sentra and Altima, as well as the hot-selling Ford Focus.

The Lancer, in its early U.S. version and the higher performance Evolution model released in 2003, does offer a remarkable value – especially in terms of style for dollars. Potential buyers need only deal with some less-than-Honda-like build quality. However, the payoff is a quick sedan that exudes fashion. The Evolution model will humble any Civic.

The Return of Nissan

While the rest of the world caught on to the sport compact craze, Nissan seemed to be content with making a 180-degree turn and running for cover. Once a mainstay of the growing market, Nissan abandoned all the disciplines that endeared them to the first wave of enthusiasts. As the interest in sport compacts began to take shape, Nissan's Sentra was one of the three most popular cars at shows, autocross races, and other related events. Slowly, the market turned away from Nissan, despite the fact that the SE-R model was one of the more potent offerings of its time. In recent years Nissan has made a major resurgence and is working hard to recapture a market that left it behind a decade earlier.

Much of the rise, fall, and rise again of Nissan can be traced back to the company's internal thought process. From the early 1970s through the mid-1990s Nissan offered the type of vehicle that could be taken in a number of personal directions. Then, almost overnight, Nissan's entire product planning team lost their way. The cars were seemingly targeted to a marketplace that was not in the same world as Honda, Mazda, Ford, or even Toyota.

Entering the twenty-first century, Nissan regained its street-smart roots and started to produce enthusiast-style cars. Beginning with the restyled Maxima, followed by the Sentra (including the return of the SE-R version), and a slick, European-styled Altima, Nissan has returned to prominence.

It took the sport compact car market to gain a bit of gray hair before the upscale Maxima could be a viable option. Early in the process Nissan offered the luxury sedan with a torque-filled V-6 and an optional manual five-speed transmission. However, while the Sentra SE-R was sticker-priced under $13,000, Maximas were venturing into the $20-grand neighborhood. A few years on the used car market meant the same Maxima could be had for the price of a new Sentra. As soon as it made more financial sense, Maximas started popping up in customized form. However, the mature styling has kept the four-door on the fringe of the movement.

What has proven to be an easy middle ground between the entry-level Sentra and the top-of-the-line Maxima is the Altima. In its showroom form the model has a little too much grandma appeal. However, add tires, wheels, performance springs, and a rear deck wing and you're ready to cruise. In the power department, Altimas share many similar components with Sentra and Maxima models, making bolt-on horsepower gains easily achieved.

Over the years Nissan's line-up has not received the attention of Honda and Acura. However, the brand has and will continue to be a smart alternative to its more popular Japanese rivals.

This old-school Sentra is a prime example of Sentra-mania from the early days of sport compact cars. Note the "way cool" 15-inch wheels and chromed gas filler door–high-tech in 1992.

Toying With Success

Based on the sheer size and strength of the company, one would have thought that Toyota would be sitting atop the sport compact kingdom. This is not the case, although it's not from lack of effort. It has been more a lack of direction that has kept Toyota from challenging Honda for the crown.

In terms of total vehicles sold, Toyota is light years ahead of Honda. This is mainly due to the 40-year head start Toyota has in selling trucks and sport utility vehicles. On the enthusiast front Toyota of America executives are far behind Honda.

This is not to say that some very well-designed and well-engineered cars haven't gone down the road with the Toyota emblem attached to the trunk lid. Many excellent sport compacts are Toyota models, such as the MR2, Supra, and Celica. Due to marketing image and price positioning, none of the aforementioned models have stepped up to challenge the offerings from Honda, or even Nissan.

Two of Toyota's trio of performance cars are of the two-seat variety (covered in chapter 3). The lone sport coupe is the Celica, which has been a consistent performer since its introduction in the mid-1970s.

Nissan returned to its performance ways at the dawn of the new millennium. The road was nearly complete with the new 2000 SE-R. Each year the little racer offers more thrills for fewer bills.

Toyota's Celica was the pioneer of the pure import sport coupe. As the model evolved, Toyota continued to build in improved overall performance, combining acceleration, handling, and drivability. The downside to the Celica could always be found in the sticker price. Toyota had a knack for pricing its cars just above its close competitors. However, there was an upside. The larger buy-in was equal to the horsepower and suspension sophistication it delivered.

When Toyota debuted its all-new Celica in 2000, it raised the import sport coupe bar to an entirely new level. When compared directly to the Eclipse GT and Civic Si, the results were clearly in Celica's favor. As a platform to build on, all the speed and cosmetic components are available. In line with the higher sticker price, most of the accessories will also set you back an average of 10 percent over similar products for the Civic Si.

The Celica is not the only non-two-seat Toyota to enjoy acceptance in the sport compact

When the 2000 Celica was unveiled at Toyota dealerships, it created the wow-factor the quiet giant was hoping for. Its power and handling quickly made the sports coupe a sought-after performer and feared competitor.

Toyota added to its youth market vehicle line with the Matrix. The Japanese carmaker and *Sport Compact Car* magazine combined to create this 2003 version featuring an XS Engineering turbo and Vishnu Performance engine management system to bring the engine output to 250horsepower. *Toyota*

world. Corolla, Tercel, and Paseo models each produced a following, although slight in comparison. Each of these models served as preludes to the eventual goal of tricking out a Celica.

Toyota does own the distinction of having the one nameplate that has successfully crossed over from the truck world to the sport compact crowd. The Tacoma, with help from Toyota Racing Development (TRD), with its basic 2.3 liter engine and solid rear-wheel-drive configuration, has been very capable drag race combination. TRD features a wide array of go-fast parts (many originally designed for use on off-road race trucks) that can easily transform a Tacoma into an asphalt-kicking, tire-smoking strip blazer. And, because the initial buy-in cost is lower than nearly all coupes and sedans, the desired results can be achieved at a lower overall cost.

Zoom-Zoom – Image vs. Reality

Mazda's catchy buzz song "Zoom-Zoom" was developed to enhance the idea that Mazda made fun, zoomy performers with "the soul of a sports car." Somehow a tune was going to convince consumers that mini-vans, SUVs, and trucks were designed and built with the same commitment to enthusiast driving as the Miata. While this worked to elevate Mazda's consumer status, the truth is that to many executives Zoom-Zoom was more than an advertising campaign – it was a mission statement.

Leaving the Miata for the next chapter, Mazda's attitude helped produce a number of very slick cars. The most notable are the Protégé and the Protégé 5—a pair with plenty of potential—and the larger 6 sedan.

Timing is everything in life, and Mazda displayed an ideal understanding of this hard-to-grasp quality with its introduction of the Protégé. As the 2001 Civic reached the market, the change in styling and suspension configuration produced a backlash from enthusiasts. This consumer double-take created a market for enthusiasts looking for the next cool alternative. For many the answer was the Protégé.

Mazda turned the heat up in 2001 with the release of the limited edition MP3 version and the sweet styling of the Protégé 5, which was quickly renamed by the street crowd as the Pro 5.

Working in cooperation with key aftermarket companies, Mazda launched the MP3 as an example of what could be done. In the fall of 2002, Mazda launched its first factory hot rod—the Mazdaspeed Protégé—using the same principles. Beginning with the base model, all the right pieces have become available to turn the Protégé into a Civic-beater.

The success story of the Protégé 5 is much the same. This sports-wagon combines excellent enthusiast potential with added room. At first one might think, "Hey, who needs the extra air space." However, if you're a fan of big audio, the shell of the Pro 5 provides a very slick sound chamber, allowing sound to resonate and reverberate. Not only can a Pro 5 be built to scream, it can also *scream* at the same time.

Mazda's Protégé 5 gained instant acceptance in the sport compact car world and has helped establish Mazda as a force to be reckoned with. The smooth sport-wagon design and modifiable platform, along with factory-backed performance parts availability, has pushed sales to enthusiasts beyond the carmaker's projections. *Mazda*

▼ THE ONES

1973 RX-2: Cult car that can be built to drive circles around 5.0 Mustangs.

1990 MX-3 V-6: Slaphappy V-6 power and a tight suspension.

2000 Protégé: Mazda finally offers a sedan with star quality.

2001 Protégé 5: Supersweet styling on an outstanding platform.

What Mazda started with Zoom-Zoom has spread to its MPV mini-van, Tribute SUV, and 6 sedan. Each have a little of the Miata and Protégé spirit. Honda won the early enthusiast market without trying. Mazda's efforts at the turn of the twenty-first century has eroded Honda's stranglehold on the market as the Protégé joined the Civic on the short lists of sport compact enthusiasts.

If you've got an extra $50,000 lying around, you could duplicate this super tuner Protégé. Under the hood of this Mandarin Orange Pearl sedan is a 240 horsepower, turbocharged engine that moves the 1,000-watt audio system along at a rapid pace.

The Power of the Blue Oval

Built on a firm foundation of performance and racing, Ford has long been the American automaker capable of challenging all players in the enthusiast's marketplace. From the birth of the sport compact car interest, Ford has been on the front lines. In the late 1980s the Escort was one of the big three models on the scene (along with the Nissan Sentra and Honda Civic).

Ford paraded the Escort as the World Car and, on a global level, out-sold every car, becoming more popular than the Volkswagen Beetle. As a performance car, the GT model offered more aggressive suspension components, increased horsepower and smooth-looking trim pieces. The price was low and the value was high. This set the trend for Ford to far outdistance its domestic rivals (Chevrolet and Dodge) for street and show presence.

Ford raised the stakes with the introduction of the Probe in 1988 and later with a 2.2 liter turbocharged GT version featuring decent horsepower in an oddly attractive shell. Although the motor didn't produce a lot of boost, the forced-induction Probe ushered in a performance attitude that helped change the face of sport compacting, pushing it from slammed suspension, wild paint, and big audio to advanced handling and acceleration.

The Probe has become a small footnote in the market as Ford killed off the model in favor of the more sellable Contour. This proved to be a far more popular offering and still has a small impact on the street scene. It also spawned a go-fast, great-handling SVT version that has developed a cult following among Ford fans who usually fixate on the latest Mustang.

The most dynamic model to come from the land of the Blue Oval is the Focus. Dressed up, the ZX3 version is a serious player and represents the first real threat to hardcore Civic enthusiasts.

Right from the get-go Ford was preparing the Focus to not just challenge Honda's Civic, but to dethrone the sport compact king. As early as

Ford created a positive market impact with the Focus. Strong factory support resulted in instant editorial and industry acceptance. Enthusiasts started building slick street versions within hours of the coupe's 1999 release.

1998, Focus platform engineers were secretly creating a street version that would catapult the image and desire for the ZX3 version. Debuted on the SuperStreet Tour and at the NOPI Nationals, the project whet the appetite of the 50,000 participants and spectators. When the Focus ZX3 hit the dealer's showroom a few months later, demand was nearly overwhelming. The performance aftermarket played a willing accomplice in the early surge with everything from special dash fascias to coil-over spring kits ready to go from day one.

As Ford hoped, the Focus has become a cornerstone of the sport compact car world. The platform is an outstanding performer right off the lot and is rivaled only by the Civic and Miata when it comes to availability of performance and cosmetic aftermarket enhancements.

Chrysler's second generation Neon features additional power and refinement, as well as more sophisticated suspension components. The R/T model is an excellent platform on which to build.

▼ THE ONES

1988-89 Escort GT: One of the original power brokers in the sport compact movement. More horsepower over previous year (115) and improved suspension and interior features.
1991 Probe GT: Factory turbo power and a decent suspension package. Better styling.
1997 Probe GT: Now with 164 horsepower and updated styling.
1998 Contour: Best compact sedan to come from Ford yet.
1999 Escort ZX2: Slick upgrade from the old Escort platform. Very affordable.
2001 Focus ZX3: The first car to really challenge the Civic. All the right aftermarket stuff available.

Pentastar Persuasion

Since the end of World War II, Chrysler has been a performance car force. Always displaying a knack for understanding car enthusiasts, Chrysler's nameplates have produced an army of fast cars. However, the strength of Dodge, Plymouth, and Chrysler has been grounded in mega-monster V-8 engines (with the notable exception of the Viper's V-10).

Since 1982 Chrysler has made several attempts to capture the hearts and minds of sport compact car enthusiasts with the Daytona, Shadow, and Omni. The Neon was the eventual winner the Sterling Heights, Michigan, company was longing for.

Released as twins under the Dodge and Plymouth banners, Neons made a splash but suffered from questionable build quality and a limited number of performance and cosmetic aftermarket components. Try as it might, Chrysler could not get the Neon to the mainstream in critical regions of the sport. In the West, the stronghold of Hondaism, Neons were not a factor on the street or on the strip. However, in the Northeast and Southeast,

Dodge/Plymouth worked diligently to break the first generation Neon into the sport compact car scene. This version is indicative of how early Neons can be effectively outfitted on a budget. It features 16-inch Ts & Ws, performance springs, sunroof, cold air intake, header, performance exhaust, styling package, racing seats, short shifter, bigger anti-sway bars, and traditional Dodge racing stripes. The entire car can be built on a budget of less than $6,000.

Neons were looked upon as a viable and cost-effective alternative to the Civic.

After the Plymouth name was retired, Dodge owned the Neon nameplate and quickly used its R/T heritage to bring a higher horsepower version to the street wars. As the ball in Times Square dropped on 2001, Neon R/T raised the consciousness of sport compacters and began to ask the question, "Why not a Neon?"

When Chrysler introduced the PT Cruiser in 2000, it was designed to attract a sport compact element. However, the race to the dealers to snatch the early offerings was won by a different demographic. All too soon the roadways were full of gray-haired PT drivers. This effectively put the skids on sport compact car enthusiasts, who avoided being associated with a car that soccer moms drive. This is not to say that a few PTs haven't made their way into the fold – it's just not as heavy as Chrysler execs predicted.

1983 Dodge Rampage: Unique styling, good horsepower, low production numbers.
1986 Dodge Daytona Turbo Z: Surprising power, cool styling.
1986 Chrysler Laser XT: Little-known model with plenty of power.
1989 Chrysler Conquest Tsi: Power way ahead of its time, cool shape, great handling.
1994 Neon: After a few years of trying, this model was ready to rock.
2001 Dodge Neon R/T: All the right stuff to build a Civic Si buster.
2003 PT Cruiser GT: Turbo power and all the cool do-dads to make it sweet.

Frigginmovin'

Throughout the 1990s, sport compacting was dominated by Japanese brands, with Ford and Chrysler making small dents in the exterior. However, there was another force at work—that

Chrysler hoped the PT Cruiser would play a role in the sport compact movement. The crossover vehicle, however, seemed to create its own enthusiasts' niche. Some owners of sport compact-style PTs are slowly working their way into the mainstream.

When the new Beetle started showing up at dealers, sport compact enthusiasts ate up the early inventory. Impact slowed nearly as quickly as the soft interior and exterior styling labeled the Beetle as a "chick" car.

of the German variety.

Volkswagen has maintained a constant presence in the compact car market, even before the "sport" was put before the "compact." Relying on its reputation for superior engineering and handling, VW models have a very loyal following.

We all know that Volkswagen made its mark with the air-cooled Beetle. However, beginning in 1975 VW flip-flopped its philosophy and converted to the traditional water-cooled engine. The front-wheel-drive Rabbit and Scirocco models blew into town just as the consumer base transitioning from GM, Ford, and Chrysler were finding that the prices of Datsuns, Toyotas, and Hondas were getting hard to stomach. The introduction of the European rivals was ideally timed.

It wasn't until 1983 that the words *performance* and *water-cooled* could be linked together in a VW. With the GTI and Scirocco, VW carved out its own little niche in a tuner market that had yet to be invented or identified.

In 1990 the street heat was turned up when the Scirocco was retired and the Corrado arrived on American soil. The Golf-platform-based model featured the G60 with a supercharged 1.8 liter engine that served up 160 horsepower and 0–60 mph under 7.5 seconds. The advanced aerodynamics and usable ergonomics set the Corrado head and shoulders above the competition.

The big VW popularity jump came in 1993 with the release of the Jetta and Golf. These two rockets helped create the need for even more advanced aftermarket performance components for its Japanese rivals. In factory form the acceleration, handling, and drivability were miles ahead of small cars from America or Japan. This was further emphasized when the VR6 started burning up pavement.

VW sales and popularity rolled along at a consistent pace from 1993 to 1997, never challenging Honda and Toyota, nor losing ground to Ford, Mazda, and Mitsubishi. This changed in 1998 when the New Beetle brought a new market presence to the VW name. Suddenly it was very hip to drive a VW. Although the New Beetle sold reasonably well, the reincarnation really helped sell Passats, GTIs, and Jettas.

The strong VW aftermarket no doubt enhanced the popularity of VWs. There has never been a shortage of speed or glamour parts available for any VW model. The current line of VeeDubs is no different.

Released in 2003, the Beetle Cabriolet and the Passat W8 further expand the reach of VW. Whatever the model, VW continues to hold the interest of a core group of compact car enthusiasts.

The Passat line can also pull off the street racer look without looking forced or cheesy.

▼ THE ONES

1985 GTI: Fun, fast, and cheap.
1989 Scirocco: Final year, more refined, makes good club racer.
1991 Rabbit Cabriolet: Classic styling, good "chick" appeal.
1992 Corrado G60: Great handling, cool styling, low production numbers.
1994 GTI VR6: Rocket ship on four wheels.
1998 New Beetle: Very cool once tricked out.
2000 Passat: Luxury, style, performance – it's got it all.
2001 Turbo Beetle: Improved power, smooth turbo transition.
2002 GTI: Best of the GTI offerings.
2003 Beetle Cabriolet: Modern day classic.
2003 Passat W8: Once you get over sticker shock, it's a world-class sedan.

The Other Guys

Thus far, just about all the coupes and sedans have been covered. However, there are a number of bit players yet to be discussed. These are makes and models that are in the game, just less significantly.

The most notable brand name missing from the prior pages is Chevrolet. Since the Vega, Chevy has never found its sport compact stride. The Bow Tie party has had few sport compact success stories. Chevy has tried to push Cavalier since the early days of the movement. Prior to 1988 (the unofficial start of the sport compact car niche), Chevy offered a sporty Z/24 model featuring a potent 135 horsepower V-6. However, despite a price tag similar to with Ford's Escort GT, the Cavalier never struck a chord with enthusiasts. Chevy held on to the shape and platform much too long and captured virtually no share of the sport compact market. It still doesn't.

Throughout the early 1990s selected Chevy dealers did have sport compact traffic with the introduction of the GEO brand. This was a mixture of vehicles built in partnership with three other manufacturers: Toyota, Isuzu, and Suzuki. Two models showed a flash of street glory, the pint-sized Metro and the slick-styled Storm. The Metro was a tiny subplayer and lasted as long as the convertible ragtop would

Many models that were on track to be staple items in sport compacting turned out to be nothing more than a flash in the pan. The Geo Storm was one such nameplate. When introduced in 1989 it found a quick following, one that faded just as rapidly.

operate. The Storm, however, enjoyed a more lasting presence, even making the cover of *Sport Compact Car* magazine in October 1992. Never a quick runner (90 horsepower), the real appeal was the cutting-edge exterior styling and ease of modification.

The following three makes and models represent the upper crust of the two- and four-door compact car scene. BMW (3-Series), Lexus (IS300), and Infiniti (G20) have been in a low-level battle for enthusiasts looking to upscale their driving pleasure while, at the same time, looking to retain acceptance with the rest of the sport compact crowd.

Of these three models BMW 3-Series sedans have the longest pedigree, dating back to 1977. The model continued to improve throughout the decades, changing form and function with each new generation. Its strength has always been the ideal balance of power and handling, providing the driver with remarkable feedback and motoring confidence.

Jumping into the fold in 1991, the Infiniti G20 shares components with its Nissan cousin, the Sentra. Always offered in a more refined package, the G20 has enjoyed enduring, although limited, success. Platform changes in 2000 improved handling, but the entire exercise was overshadowed when Lexus released its IS300 a year later.

Striking an instant chord with sport compacters, the Lexus IS300 has been both a sales and image success for Toyota's luxury car division. The first year the rear-wheel drive sedan offered an excellent power-to-weight ratio and a five-speed automatic with manual slap shifting. The road-going manners rival that of the BMW 330. Horsepower comes from a 3-liter in-line six cylinder producing 215 ponies. A year later Lexus became even more aggressive by mating a smooth-shifting five-speed manual gearbox to the high-revving six. Also added to the line was the very hip SportCross five-door model.

▼ THE ONES

1990 BMW 320: Balanced handling, excellent power.
1992 Infiniti G20: Luxury in a small, modifiable package.
1994 BMW 318ti: Cool hatchback styling, remarkably affordable.
1999 Infiniti G20: New power and improved handling.
2002 Lexus IS300: Quick, cool, and five forward manual gears.

On the upper end of the scale is the BMW line of coupes, sedans, and convertibles. While market depreciation brings the buy-in fees closer to reality, the price tag can be steep. The upside to all BMWs is knowing you've got a platform that will likely meet even the most lofty ideals and anticipations.

Notably absent from chapter 2 were all the two-seaters and sports cars that have wormed their way into the sport compact car world. While automotive historians will want to make a case for Alfa-Romeo, Fiat, Porsche, MG, Triumph, and Lotus, automotive historians likely haven't got a clue of what's happening in our gear slamming, tire smokin' world.

Instead, the focus of this chapter will be on the 1+1 cars that have made (and continue to make) an impact on sport compacting. These include models from Mazda, Honda, Nissan, Toyota, Mitsubishi, and even Mercury.

Sports cars are not for everyone, although nearly everyone can see themselves driving a sports car. These are the cars that evoke an undeniable spirit – promoting a oneness with the road. The romance of driving is what makes the impractical configuration of a sports car a justifiable purchase. These are the vehicles of emotional escape – beckoning us to enjoy the pure, unadulterated pleasure of driving.

Mazda Reinvents the Market

Modern-day sports cars (manufactured after 1948) are by no means a new idea. However, in

What was originally intended to provide basic transportation to a college-bound generation turned into a two-seater with cult-car status. Honda's CRX is one of those rare vehicles that has found a permanent home within the automotive community. All years and variants of the Honda CRX are in demand. Some tuners take it to the streets; others build show versions, while many find the platform perfect for autocross competition.

Miatas lend themselves to full modifications, such as this gen one, featuring a full bag of items including a big-boost turbo package, coil-over suspension, even Honda motorcycle side mirrors. This car has been a consistent show winner since 1999.

1989, the entire idea of the personal sports car was reborn when Mazda introduced the Miata. Prior to August of that year, the affordable sports car market was declining, in both sales and available models. Long-gone were former icons MG, Triumph, and Fiat. Lotus was on its last legs and Alfa Romeo had prepared to pull out of the U. S. market. But Mazda not only had a good marketing plan, it also had designed the best low-cost sports car ever made.

Many factory improvements were made when the second generation Miata debuted for 1999. This version is supercharged and has been known to run door-to-door with many Honda S2000 and BMW Z3 rivals. In addition, the St. Louis-based street beast has made cross-country runs without worries.

Mazda brought true super-car status to the third-generation RX-7. The twin-rotor, twin turbo-charged two-seater was described by leading auto publications as being "bike fast." At the time of its release it could easily out-accelerate Corvettes, Ferraris, and Porsches. *Mazda*

Right out of the gate the Miata was a boon to the auto world. Sport compact car enthusiasts were slow to get into the act due to the extreme difficulty of securing the model from dealerships. Miatas were selling at a furious pace for thousands of dollars over sticker price, taking the car out of the price range of younger buyers. Within a few years the tide changed and Miatas crept into the sport compact mainstream.

The Miata has experienced several evolutions, gaining some power and weight along the way. During its short history the Miata compelled BMW, Honda, Toyota, Audi, and Nissan to get into (or return to) the two-seat sports car field.

As a performance car, the Miata rivals the Civic as the most modifiable platform in today's street and sport scenes. Everything you can imagine, from pneumatic cup-holders to V-8 conversion kits, can be had.

The Rotary Club

The Miata's big, all-powerful brother was the RX-7. Mazda failed to market the car in a successful manner during its best version (in terms of quality and power) from 1993–95. The third generation RX-7 was, and still is, considered by many to be one of the best all-around sports cars ever manufactured.

The first gen RX-7 (1978–85) was revolutionary for its time. While the car developed a loyal following, it has never had an impact on the sport compact world. The larger, heavier, and more powerful 1986–91 RX-7 does enjoy slightly more acceptance. This is largely due to the available variations. It was made in coupe and convertible form—with a 200 horsepower turbo-charged coupe as the go fastest version.

High priced at the time of its release (starting at $32,000 in 1993 and finishing at $42,000 in 1995), the third-gen RX-7 was a world-class performer with acceleration that was likened to that of a high-performance motorcycle. The twin-rotor, twin-turbocharged rotary engine was reported to generate 255 horsepower. Dyno-testing revealed that in factory trim the rating was more a rear-wheel reading than a flywheel measurement.

What keeps the final-generation RX-7 so popular is the power potential of the car.

With basic upgrades the 13B engine can pump out 400 to 500 horsepower with 350-450ft-lb of torque. The most common problem was thought to be the failure of the primary turbo. It has been discovered, however, that this ailment is often no more than rotting vacuum lines. Prices for generation three RX-7s have remained high—much higher than that of the previous two models.

▼ BEST PICKS
1989-91 Turbo Coupe: Nice styling, turbo power, good quality.
1991 Convertible: Sweet styling, low wind noise, very affordable.
1995: Best of the best. Quality issues worked out. Very fast.

The European Miata

BMW's Z3 started out as a European-styled rival to the Miata, but quickly became an over-priced, over-grown sports car that remains beyond the radar screen of sport compacters. The first releases were good looking, but slow and priced nearly $10,000 above the Miata. In 1996-1997, the 138 horsepower four-cylinder version offered ten additional ponies over the Miata, but gave back 500 pounds in weight. Thus the acceleration of the two roadsters was equal. The big difference was that you can add a supercharger, exhaust, performance springs, and shocks to a Miata and still have money left over and blow the Z3 off the road on the way to the bank.

Later BMW corrected its errors by offering six-cylinder engines from the 3-series, with a top horsepower of 240 in 2002. The price also grew with the horsepower, keeping the Z3 a rich man's compact two-seater.

With the Fall 2002 introduction of the BMW Z4, the previous Z3 model became affordable to a larger segment of sport compact car enthusiasts. The later model, especially 3.0 liter versions, is a very potent machine, although short on aftermarket upgrades.

Honda cut the del Sol from its line in 1997 due to shrinking demand. The ability to install many bolt-on performance parts from Civics of the same age makes the del Sol a sporty alternative to a coupe or sedan grocery-getter.

Honda's Cult Car

Honda's two-seater lineup has scored one win, one loss, and one tie. On the winning side is the CRX. As one of the early icons of the sport, the CRX has become a staple model of sport compacting. Arriving in 1984, the CRX was *Motor Trend* magazine's Car of the Year. It ushered in a new attitude at Honda that proclaimed that Honda could produce fun, sporty cars that would appeal to a growing number of youthful buyers. Although underpowered (58 horsepower) in 1984, Honda

followed up in 1985 with an Si model that pushes the 1,713-pound racer with an improved 91 horsepower. All CRX models, particularly the Si versions, are highly sought after and will always be a cornerstone of sport compacting.

Honda's Gamble

Released in 1993 as a replacement for the CRX, the Honda del Sol never caught on with sports car nuts who were in the middle of a love affair with Mazda's Miata. Sport compacters have discovered that the del Sol is a unique alternative to a Civic. Based on the

A Honda without limits is the best way to describe the S2000. The high-revving engine is capable of producing unreal high-end speed with Honda reliability. With the vast amount of aftermaket products that can be had, the S2000 is a model that begs to be played with.

same platform, the final-year del Sol Si was fitted with the 160-horsepower VTEC engine. As a street car, the del Sol makes a slick and capable road warrior.

▼ BEST PICKS

1996-1997 Si: Strong VTEC engine. Low production numbers.

Honda's Halo

In late 1999 Honda released the two-seater that would become its halo vehicle well into the year 2005—the S2000. This is a street car that revs like a Formula 1 racer. Power for the roadster comes from a 2.0 liter four-cylinder engine with massive power (120 horsepower per liter), much of it over 5,000 rpm. The S2000 engine thrives in territory where other engines go to die.

Where the S2000 loses points in the sport compact scene is the price of admission. Nearly every Honda dealer in North America used the S2000 to gain additional profits, adding monster premiums to the bottom line and pushing the price into Corvette range. Another good/bad thing about the S2000 is that the car is almost perfect right off the showroom floor. Even adding a supercharger to the car—while adding as much as 100 horsepower—seems to throw off the car's ideal balance.

The S2000 handles so well the need for aftermarket springs, anti-sway bars, and adjustable shocks is minimal. There are some cosmetic changes that do make sense—gauges, higher quality leather seating surfaces, audio, and more aggressive tires and wheels.

▼ BEST PICKS

2000-present: It's all good.

Toyota's Oriental Roman

In 1985 Toyota introduced its first generation MR2 sports car. This was the automaker's first imported two-seater. (Toyota manufactured the 2000GT from 1965–70 and the smaller 800 from 1968–73). The initial U. S. spec sports car was also the first Toyota featuring a mid-engine design. The engine was the same 112-horsepower unit carried over from the Corolla sedan.

Unlike its two rivals of the day, the Pontiac Fiero and Fiat X1/9, the MR2 was a completely reliable go-cart. Many owners of exotic sports cars, such as Ferraris, Lamborghinis, and Panteras purchased MR2s as daily drivers.

The most popular of all the MR2 models was generation two, offered from 1991–95. The mini-Ferrari styling and superb power-to-weight ratio have made the car an envied and revered model among sport compacters. If you're into the second gen MR2, be prepared to pony up because prices remain strong because desire for these cars has not waned.

Tricking out a 1991–95 MR2 is quite easy. The aftermarket responded en masse to the car, and parts remain readily available, although little is needed to make these cars run strong and corner tight. Great improvements were made in driver positioning, visibility, and power over the first MR2. The 1991–95 MR2 is also a much more palatable platform for all forms of the market—from street, to strip, to sport, or to show.

The new generation MR2 Spyder, with its awkward cheese-cutter styling and sawed-off rear deck, combined with an interior that was crafted from whatever Toyota had left in its parts bins, has kept the car from being the

One of the most aesthetically pleasing automobiles to come from a Japanese design studio (sport or otherwise) was the second-generation Toyota MR2. This was truly a mini-Ferrari in every sense – with the notable exception that the MR2 was completely reliable and drivable on a daily basis. It also provided an excellent platform for an exceptional all-around performer – especially the later turbocharged versions. *Toyota*

After a lapse of several model years the MR2 resurfaced as part of the Toyota line. The roadster version had a new hard-edged shape, a major league departure from the Italian inspired silhouette of years earlier. The new version, although full of zip-zip (opposed to the Miata's zoom-zoom), has been slow to catch on with sport compacters.

Miata rival Toyota hoped for. While factory performance is considered good (0–60 in 7.6 seconds), aftermarket companies have found engineering bolt-on accessories difficult due to severe space constraints.

Aside from much-needed performance tires, wheels, springs, and shocks, there is not much more that can be done to seriously modify the car, which has made it a small player in the game.

> ### ▼ BEST PICKS
> **1986:** First year with optional T-roof panels.
> **1989-1990:** Perfected supercharged models with 145 horsepower and greater potential.
> **1992-1994:** Non-turbo models more affordable.
> **1993-1995:** Traction issues on 200 horsepower turbocharged models solved

Toyota's Top Gun

Toyota was not without its big gun to shoot back at its Japanese neighbors, Nissan (300ZX) and Mazda (RX-7). The best of the Supra line (1993–98) shared the same big-six engine as the Lexus SC300. The twist over the Lexus counterpart is the twin-turbo model pumping out 320 horsepower with plenty of neck-snap.

The last-generation Supra quickly achieved legendary status for its seemingly unlimited performance potential. A total of 43,000 fourth generation Supras were sold. Along with the retired RX-7, 300ZX Twin Turbo, and current Acura NSX, the Supra enjoys the distinction of being a true exotic Japanese sports cars.

> ### ▼ BEST PICKS
> **1993-98:** Twin turbo-charged model produces massive horsepower. In factory form it is far below its potential.

Nissan/Datsun established itself as a sport car innovator in the 1960s. With the release of the 1990 300ZX, the carmaker opened up the world to the thought of Japanese exotic sport cars. The Twin Turbo model was a power-stuffed asphalt kicker delivering 300 factory ponies. All the go-fast goodies are available to wring 500 horsepower out of these now affordable monsters.

Nissan's Nasty Attitude

Nissan was the first Japanese automaker to bring affordable world-class styling and performance to America. In 1989 Nissan released an all-new 1990 300ZX, a highbrow sports car with Italian styling and Japanese reliability. Like its eventual competition, Nissan made the 300ZX an overpriced exotic that quickly outgrew its customer base with ballooning pricing. Unlike the Supra and RX-7, prices for used 300ZX models quickly softened, and with it the popularity of the car rose.

Today 1990–96 300ZXs are the most common and affordable of the Japanese exotics. Of special interest are the Twin Turbo models that, in factory form, pump out 300 horsepower. Add the aftermarket factor, and the 300ZX is the most cost-effective model to build into a real Corvette-busting street burner.

Nissan built and sold more 300ZXs than final generation Supras, RX-7s, and NSXs combined. More supply means satisfiable demand, lower entry fees, and go-fast parts. All of these factors have kept the 300ZX in sport compact favor.

Exactly The Same . . . Only Different

Six years after the death of the 300ZX, Nissan returned to the sports car wars with the new 350Z. With outstanding handling and power, the 350Z's price is seemingly under its European born competition—if, indeed, the competition is Porsche and Audi.

Nissan's true sports car competition, however, is not from Germany, but from Japan. Released prior to Mazda's RX-8, the 350 grabbed the spotlight and made full use of its solo time.

A few months after its release, modified versions showed up at various sport compact events from California to the Carolinas. Although it is too early to measure the car's impact on sport compacting, it is fair to assume

Similar to Toyota bringing back the MR2, Nissan returned the Z car to its line after a six-year sleep. The newest Nissan halo quickly made a presence on the street. *Nissan*

that it will elevate Nissan's image to a level not seen since 1996, when the 300ZX was set adrift.

▼ BEST PICKS

2003 Track version: Superior handling, 280 horsepower, sweet styling.

Fantasy with Three Letters

There is a slew of other two-seaters that can be seen cruisin' the street scene on any Friday night. Of these, the Acura NSX has the greatest stare factor. The Japanese car of which fantasies are made, the NSX is this generation's Ferrari. Combining reliability with exotic styling, the NSX was the first world-class sports car that could be driven like a Ferrari or an Accord—depending on your mood. It also has

the star power of a Lamborghini and the price tag of a Viper.

The same thing that makes the NSX a fantasy car also keeps it from being within the sport compact mainstream—price. Even used NSX models rarely dip under $30,000. Although it looks fast, for the money one expects more acceleration and top-end. At twice the price of a Corvette, the NSX delivers only 75 percent of the performance, although it does so in an uncommon, rare package that draws envy and respect.

▼ BEST PICKS

1991: Lowest priced on used market, same styling as 2002 model.
1998: More power.
2001: More power, low build numbers.

One Car, Two Names

Mitsubishi and Dodge tried to become part of the Japanese exotic club with the 3000GT and Stealth Turbo models. The Stealth lasted only two model years (1991–92) before it was cut from the Dodge lineup. Mitsubishi held on until 1999 before pulling the plug on a car that never found its niche.

To the defense of both versions, either can be built to very high performance standards. The Stealth can be had very cheaply and provides an upgradable platform on which to build. The 3000GT will set you back a bit more, but offers more refinement and better visuals.

Once Nissan had broken the ice for Japanese exotic cars, Honda introduced the NSX through its Acura division and started selling the ultimate sport compact car. The NSX quickly became the dream car of a new generation of car geeks. One of the advantages of an NSX over a Ferrari was that personalizing the Acura was not only acceptable–it was expected.

CHAPTER 4

FACTORY HOT RODS

What is referred to as the Muscle Car era began in the early 1960s, back when the Beach Boys were topping the charts, Detroit ruled the American roadways with monster-powered coupes and convertibles pouring out horsepower as if there was no end to the supply of gasoline. Some 30 years later a new muscle car era began, only this time players from both sides of the Pacific Ocean entered the game. More notable was that the V-8 behemoths of the 1960s and 1970s have given way to cars powered by high-revving inline four-cylinder engines and compact sixes.

Acura Integra Type R

The most desirable and famous of the factory-built hot rods is the Acura Integra Type R. Designed as a sleeper, the otherwise stock-looking Integra is a scream to drive with slot-car like handling and surging power, especially over 5,000 rpm.

First showing up in 1997, Acura played tricks with the cam timing, pistons, and connecting rods, as well as modifying the cylinder head with hand-polished intake and exhaust ports. An aluminum oil cooler was added to maximize heat dissipation and thermal efficiency. The intake was internally polished and coated for

Carmakers from around the world have unleashed a wave of factory tuner cars. From the Integra Type R to the Dodge SRT-4, the enthusiast influence has manifested itself into a line of limited-edition street rockets.

Acura unleashed a legend with the Integra Type R. The limited edition started turning heads in 1997 and concluded with the demise of the Integra name in 2001. Critics ripped the car for its harsh ride and jagged demeanor. It's these qualities that endear the coupe to enthusiasts and make the car the perfect sport compact car platform.

greater airflow velocity, complementing the exhaust as it free flows to squeeze 195 horses from 1.8 liters of displacement.

Many weight-saving techniques were employed to improve acceleration. In addition, structural rigidity was increased, and the suspension was tuned to improve transitional response during cornering. Braking is stronger as both front and rear brakes feature larger diameter rotors and bigger calipers.

Take a standard BMW 3-Series and put in on steroids and the result is the M3. First offered only in coupe form, BMW later offered a sedan and a convertible. This early edition helped raise the youth market's awareness of BMW. *BMW*

The later M3s provided refinement and additional power. As this example points out, an aftermarket carbon-fiber hood and open exhaust translates into drag racing. Is nothing sacred? *DVimaging*

Acura intended to produce only a few thousand Type-R coupes over a two-year period. The two years turned into five model years—ending in 2001. As a side note, Acura did not offer a Type-R in 1999. Production remained limited with only 4,221 total units produced.

BMW M3

BMW jumped into the tuner market by default with the 1987 introduction of the M3. Originally designed for European Touring Car racing, the 1987–90 M3 is a sweet, boxy little Bavarian, supplying 190 horsepower with a BMW Motorsport tuned engine (thus the M designation) and responsive braking. The first generation M3 was premature for the early sport compact movement but laid the foundation as a fantasy car for everyone driving a Sentra, Escort, or GTI.

Where BMW really scored is with the 1991–2001 M3 models, although escalating prices have kept the model from being remotely affordable (it jumped over the $40,000 mark in 1998). The M3 has become *the* dream machine, a destination point on the road of life for many who currently drive anything less.

All M3s are easily identified by special styling cues. Yet the real story of the M3 series is under the hood. The more recent models featured the 3.2 liter inline six-cylinder engine with as much as 333 horsepower, capable of rocketing the M3 to quarter-mile times that rival Hemi 'Cudas of 30 years ago. Zero to 60 is accomplished in 4.9 seconds and 1,320 feet of asphalt is gobbled up in 13.6 seconds at 107 miles per hour. That's heady stuff for a compact car.

BMW has achieved this near-perfect driver's car by employing variable valve timing and individual throttle bodies for each cylinder. This allows the engine to have remarkable adaptability to changing conditions and desires. A free-flowing exhaust system adds to the engine's

In an attempt to remedy the underwhelming performance of the PT Cruiser, Chrysler released a Turbo GT version in the fall of 2002. Its 215 horsepower helped bring some measure of respectability to the car/SUV/mini-van.

efficiency. A stronger crankshaft and lighter connecting rods enable the engine to approach an 8,000 rpm redline without worry.

Chevrolet Cosworth Vega

The first factory-built compact hot rod came from Chevrolet in the unlikely form of the Vega. In 1975 and 1976, select Chevy dealers sold twin-cam Cosworth Vegas, powered by a highly-detuned aluminum-block 2.3 liter inline four engine. Capable of producing 220 horsepower, the Cosworth powerplant was computer controlled and emission device laden to a disappointing 111 horses.

A host of other special suspension and trim items set the Cosworth Vega apart from the rest of the Chevy line. True believers know the

engine's potential and can make the necessary adjustments that turn the little compact car into one of the quickest things to come out of Detroit. Total production for the two-year run was cut short at 3,508 units.

Chrysler PT Cruiser Turbo

The common, everyday PT Cruiser has found its own niche in the automotive world— far from the high energy of the sport compact crowd. In late 2002 Chrysler introduced GT version powered by a 2.4 liter engine with turbocharged induction.

Sporting 215 horsepower, the engine is shared with the new Dodge Neon SRT, although rated to have a 10 horsepower advantage over the Neon with an additional 25 pounds of peak torque. While the power was upgraded, the GT's suspension (like all PTs) requires serious upgrading to provide any resemblance of high-performance road manners.

Visually, the GT version stands out with monochromatic trim, including bumpers and chrome-plated 17-inch five spoke wheels on 205-50-17 tires. The "GT" emblem on the lower left of the rear hatch is also a dead giveaway.

It is uncertain if the PT Cruiser will ever become an accepted part of the sport compact car community. If it does, it will be the Turbo GT that leads the way.

Dodge Daytona IROC R/T

Dodge has been a force in high performance since the 1950s. However, in the sport compact car world the tried-and-true American brand has never made the impact the company's leaders wanted. In an attempt to attract buyers, a number of special vehicles were produced—one of which was the Daytona R/T.

Even by today's standards the R/T is a respectable performer. The 224 turbocharged horses—on the cutting edge of performance in 1992—are still very respectable. The stiffened suspension is indicative of the IROC R/T's race-car-with-license-plates persona. The car is demanding to drive, as the light front-wheel drive configuration, combined with the sudden turbo boost, gives the car plenty of torque steer.

The Daytona IROC R/T has much in its favor; most notably the price. This may be the best bang-for-the-buck limited, edition factory performance car you can buy, with used prices barely reaching the $5,000 mark.

Chrysler said enough is enough to letting Ford, Honda, and Mazda have all the compact car fun and introduced the 2003 Neon SRT-4. The forced-induction sedan is a trick ride in all respects. The suspension is tuned, the interior raced-out, the exterior has just a hint of rice—all in all, a street demon with exceptional potential.

Under the hood the SRT packs a turbo punch giving the car 205 factory horses. With a bit of tuning the SRT reminds the world that Chrysler helped invent factory performance.

Dodge Neon SRT-4

As Ford proclaimed to the world that it was going to take no sport compact prisoners with its Focus SVT, Chrysler was assembling a performance vehicle operation (PVO) program. The new attitude at Chrysler would be funneled through Dodge—and its first salvo would be the Neon SRT-4. Short for "street race technology"—later renamed "street and race technology"—the SRT was designed to bust up everything Ford, Honda, Acura, GM, VW, and BMW could throw onto the street.

Dodge began with an engine swap, using the 2.4- liter 4-cylinder engine used in the PT Cruiser. Added to this displacement increase is a turbocharger that brings the engine's output to an impressive 205 horsepower at 5,400 rpm and a load of torque: 220 ft-lbs. at just 2,000 rpm. Alloy wheels, aggressive styling, and a performance-tuned suspension complete the package. The SRT-4 Neon is heavier than the most factory tuner cars at 2,970 pounds, but it more than makes up for the weight in additional performance.

Released in January 2003, sources inside Dodge report that only a few thousand units are planned for each model year at a price point that is competitive with the Focus SVT and Honda Civic Si.

Ford SVT Contour

Factory hot rodding is nothing new to Ford. One could effectively argue that the car giant invented the process. Nevertheless, when compact car performance became the thing to do, Ford's SVT division stepped to the Blue Oval plate and created a Contour variant.

Tuned to deliver crisp acceleration and sure-footed handling, the SVT Contour benefits from a normally aspirated twin-cam V-6 engine rated at 200 horsepower. The smooth-revving 2.5 liter glides under everyday driving conditions but turns into a monster on command. Mated to a five-speed manual gearbox, shifting is silky-smooth.

SVT maintains an active relationship with many high-quality aftermarket manufacturers. This accounts for how Ford's toy shop can be so responsive to enthusiast markets. For example, the SVT Contour's suspension rides on Eibach-engineered springs. These, combined with thicker anti-sway bars and more aggressive dampers, flatten the corners and provide a high degree of driver confidence.

Of all the tuner sedans, past and present, the SVT Contour is at or near the top of the performance list. Production was limited to 10,000 units. Any of the three model years (1998–2000) will deliver the goods; however, a 2000 model is the one to have if you find yourself with a choice.

Ford ZX2 S/R

In 1998 Ford performed its version of a focus group study with the ZX2 S/R . It was offered only in limited numbers (sources say 2,000) and only in California, Arizona, and Nevada. The yellow coupes were fitted with a performance air intake system, Borla exhaust, B&M shifter, Eibach springs, and special 15x7 inch alloy wheels on Z-rated tires.

Ford's street scene experiment with the S/R continued with a watered-down version for 1999 and 2000. Low demand and the advent of the Focus SVT made the S/R not much more than a footnote in the market.

Ford Focus SVT

The newest big little gun from Ford's skunkworks team is its version of the Focus. Few performance coupes on the market can match the Focus SVT dollar-for-dollar. This is a superbly engineered piece of street art. At 170 horsepower it isn't the most powerful car in the contemporary performance field, but it makes up in style and drivability. SVT did not resort to forced induction to achieve the power rating—leaving that modification up to the few lucky enough to own one of these baby racers. The SVT Focus stands ahead of its peers in the transmission department. Equipped only with the Getrag 6-

One of the most important model variants to enter the sport compact car world is the SVT Focus. The 170 horsepower, highly tuned rocket is not just a factory Focus with fancy trim. SVT has engineered this Focus to run stride-for-stride with cars way out of its price range. It's a $35,000 package with a $19,000 price tag.

There's a party goin' on at Mazda's R&D facility in Irvine, California. And whenever that happens, strange things roll out. One such gala event resulted in the creation of the MazdaSpeed Protégé – a 200 horsepower (don't let the factory info fool you) turbocharged race car with license plates.

speed manual gearbox, it is wonderfully slick and offers true close-ratio shifting.

Focus SVT coupes showed up in the spring of 2002, with the addition of the five-door SVT Focus in early 2003. Ford limits production of all SVT vehicle choices to a maximum of 25,000 per year. Of that, the Focus share is estimated to be around 7,500 units.

MazdaSpeed Protégé

The speed freaks at Mazda weren't about to let their SVT stepbrothers at Ford have all the fun. (Ford owns a substantial amount of Mazda). Pushed through the corporate maze by Mazda VP Robert Davis, MazdaSpeed is Mazda North American Operation's in-house tuner shop. Weighing all the zoomy possibilities (Miata, Protégé, Protégé 5, RX8, Mazda 6),

the wild bunch partnered with aftermarket buddies at Racing Beat to develop the 2003 MazdaSpeed Protégé.

This potent four-door took over where the Protégé MP3 of 2000 left off. The MazdaSpeed version forgoes the cold-air system for true forced induction via a turbocharger. The right-foot results are 170 horsepower and 155 ft-lbs of torque. This puts it in SVT Focus territory with slightly more torque, which offsets the Protégé's 100-pound weight disadvantage. Credit to MazdaSpeed for backing up the turbo power infusion with a limited slip differential. These units go unseen and are hard to sell to nonperformance enthusiasts, but they make a huge difference during high-speed driving. Stiffer springs and anti-roll bars complete the package, as well as body accents that add flair without being cheesy.

Joining the special edition Protégé in MazdaSpeed's lineup by 2005 will be a Protégé 5, Miata, and Mazda 6.

Shelby GLH-S - Charger GLH-S - CSX

Before the term *sport compact car* was coined, old-school automotive icons Lee Iacocca and Carroll Shelby were plotting to take over the small-car performance world. If it had not been for Honda, Toyota, Ford, Volkswagen, and BMW, they might have succeeded. In all, the teamwork of Dodge and Shelby produced a trio of hot compacts that was ahead of its time.

The first of the Shelby-made Dodges was the GLH-S. Dodge's GLH ("goes like hell") was already a slick turbocharged performer. In 1986 Shelby applied a number of skunkworks tricks to the 2.2 liter engine and upped horsepower to 175, allowing the 2,300-pound hatchback to record 0–60 times under eight seconds—a major accomplishment at the time.

The downfall of the GLH-S is the crude nature of the car. It suffers from severe torque steer and annoying turbo lag. Combine this with questionable fit and finish and there is little wonder why this Shelby has yet to reach collector car status.

Over the two-year run Shelby rolled out only 500 units. Because many of today's sport compacters were yet to reach the sixth grade by 1987, most are unaware these mini-rockets even exist.

Much like the Omni-based GLH-S, the more appealing Charger version featured the more aerodynamic L-Body exterior and sportier interior. Performance was similar to the GLH-S, as many of the same components were used to produce both in 1987. Shelby produced 1,000 Charger-based units, few of which still roam the roadways.

The last of the Shelby compacts were produced in 1988 and 1989. The CSX, based on the more modern Shadow coupe, was more refined than the Omni and Charger offerings and thus was marketed in a more aggressive manner, much to the liking of participating Dodge dealers.

The innovation of Variable Nozzle Technology (VNT) solved the turbo lag problem that plagued the GLH-S and GLH-S Charger. However, torque steer was still an issue.

The CSX was a street terror capable of blasting most Mustang GTs and Z28 Camaros off the road. Acceleration was confirmed at a lightning quick 0–60 time of 7.0 seconds. Talented drivers learned how to handle the automatic lane changes caused by stomping on the accelerator.

Shelby squeezed out 2,250 CSX models before its relationship with Chrysler took a 10-year hiatus. In the current market, a CSX (if you can find one) will likely be bargain priced. Questionable build quality and lack of replacement parts have kept the CSX from being the cult hero the CRX and Civic Si have become.

Subaru WRX

Oddly, one of the most important cars to come from the sport compact movement did not come from one of the more likely sources, but from small, obscure Subaru. The WRX is one of the most revered and feared cars in our special world. Packing all-wheel drive with a turbocharged 2.0 liter four banger, the WRX generates 227 horsepower without turbo lag and massive torque steer.

Everything about the WRX seems special. The brakes are better than anything in the factory hot rod category with 11.4-inch ventilated rotors up front and 10.3-inch solid discs in the rear. This gives the WRX stopping power to go from 60–0 in just 115 feet.

As if all the factory go-fast, handle-great stuff wasn't enough, the aftermarket rapidly responded to the WRX, producing components that allowed horsepower levels to easily reach the supercar territory.

Where Subaru differed from the others is in production. While the other factory hot rods were produced in very limited numbers, Subaru pumped out at least 10,000 WRXs per year. Good build quality and world rally durability ensures that the WRX will be an idolized part of the scene for many years.

Volkswagen Beetle Turbo S

In 2002 Volkswagen brought to America the Beetle Turbo S, a version it hoped would help overcome the "chick" factor the public quickly attached to the car. This 180 horsepower exhaust spinner brought respectable performance to the heretofore "ladies'" car.

Subaru earned the respect of the entire sport compact world with the WRX. This all-wheel-drive turbo pavement eater is available in both sedan and wagon versions. This example has been enhanced with performance exhaust, intake, suspension springs, tires, wheels, and (of course) stickers. *DVimaging*

Almost completely stealthy in appearance (only a small "Turbo S" script on the rear deck is a giveaway), the Turbo S is thankfully far more ill-mannered than its older sister. Once in motion, the Turbo S goes from 0–60 in 7.5 seconds and can reach 130 miles per hour (more if you can get around the electronically governed limiter). Upon acceleration a speed-activated rear wing slowing employs from the area between the roofline and rear window.

The Turbo S has styling cues borrowed from the aftermarket, such as stainless steel foot pedals, brushed aluminum interior trim and a tri-spoke steering wheel wrapped in special leather.

Available with the 1.8 liter turbo-assisted engine is a six-speed manual transmission, something new from VW. Like the PT Cruiser GT and Subaru WRX, production of the Beetle Turbo S will likely be higher than expected.

Volkswagen now has a chick car with a bad attitude… the Turbo Beetle. With 180 horsepower, the forced-induction flower carrier delivers the goods at a rate of 0-60 in 7.5 seconds. This is also the first Beetle to offer six forward speeds and the potential to drive an egg at 130 miles per hour. *Volkswagen*

CHAPTER 5

THE MODS

As presented earlier, the makes, models, and attitudes of the cars involved in sport compacting are vast and varied. The common modifications for each, however, are remarkably similar.

The foundation for nearly all sport compact car modifications is the suspension. Gaining the right stance is the first and foremost concern. Enthusiasts new to the sport quickly believe that lower is better. This, however, is a myth. In fact, for most vehicles, too low means too slow, no handling, and more frequent trips to the kidney dialysis ward of your local hospital. Remember, just because a car looks like a race car doesn't mean it will perform like one. For this reason performance springs have become the buzz over lowering springs. The absolute worst solution is cutting or heat setting the original factory springs.

Coordinating the suspension is important. Therefore, when performance springs are installed so should properly dampened shocks. More experienced sport compact car owners realize the harmonious value of a spring and shock combination. Newbies, on the other hand, find out the hard way. In the first place, low-buck spring cutting creates severe danger, as spring integrity is compromised. Next the factory shocks blow out because the shocks are

Tuning a sport compact car provides complete creative freedom. Builders continue to push the styling and performance envelopes in a world where anything goes and the cars often do exactly that—go.

set for normal travel. When the spring height and rate are changed, the shocks' ability to control the compression and rebound of the spring must also be upgraded in order to handle the weight and travel of the tires and wheels.

Speaking of tires and wheels, this is the next most upgraded area on a sport compact. In fact, for some, tires, wheels, and springs are as far as they go—leaving the rest of the car factory equipped.

Tires and wheels come in a wide variety of sizes, finishes, and weights. Picking the right combo has always proven to be one of the most (if not *the* most) difficult decisions you will make in the process of outfitting your sport compact. For example, if your goal is to run around cones at autocross events, large 18–19–inch wheels will slow you down. The same holds true on the drag strip. Large diameter beauty wheels are excellent for show points and street

Lower is not always better. Performance springs and shocks are designed to deliver improved handling capabilities – the look should be a bonus. The stance of this Protégé is enhanced by the addition of subtle fender flares that wrap over the tire and wheel combo.

presence, but are often the difference between winning and losing on the track. To solve this dilemma, some serious sport compact car owners have two sets of Ts and Ws—one for show and one for go.

Audio enhancements were an important factor in the early days of sport compacting. This was largely due to the absence of performance parts being developed and offered for a wide range of makes and models. The field of sound has widened to encompass sound, security, telematics, and on-board entertainment.

The magic formula involves finding the ideal connection between tires wheels and springs. The relationship of the three is vital when constructing a sport compact that will play on the street and at the track.

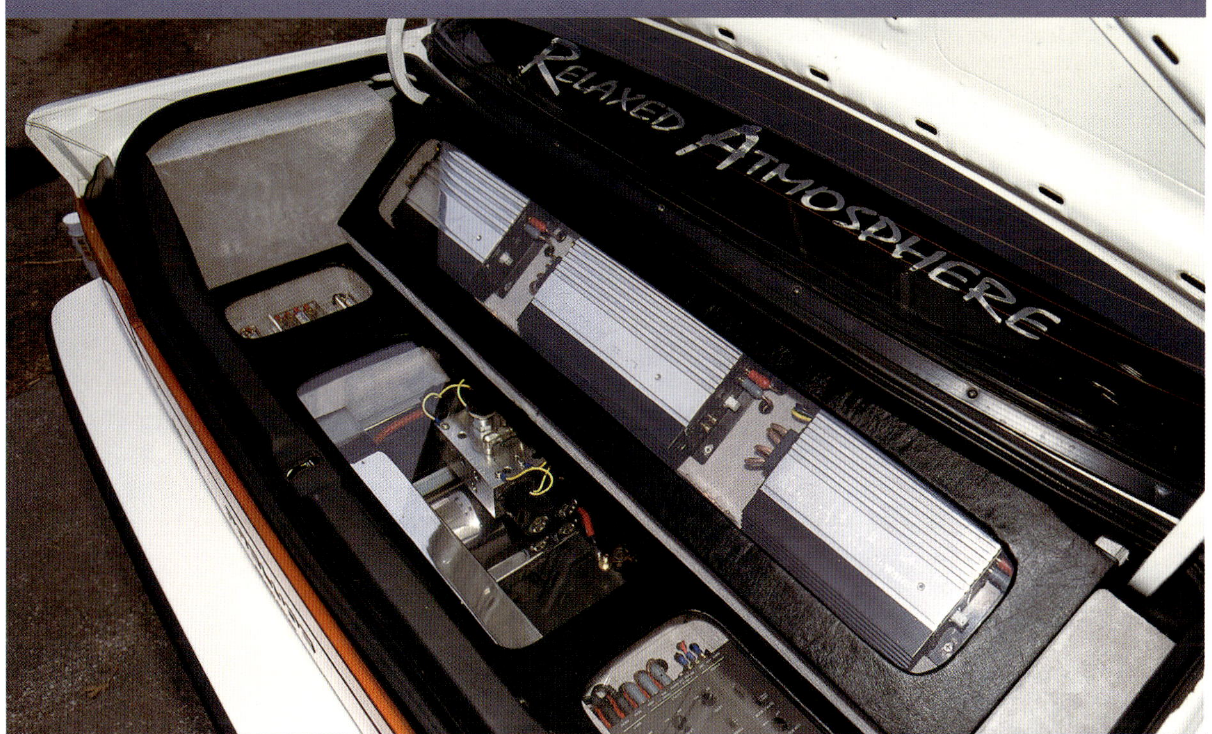

Power comes in decibels as well as horsepower. There is an entire sub-culture of the sport compact car world that measures performance by the watt. For this group, suspension modifications are just as important, as the additional weight changes the drivability of the car. Big audio dynamite costs big dough, but can return major status dividends.

Basic factory engineered car audio systems have improved vastly over the years. This has led to a change in enthusiasts' direction, from massive-watt systems with enormous speaker housings, to more space- and sound-efficient components.

Auto electronic systems can provide improved sound, but come with the compromise of added weight and reduced passenger or luggage space. When adding audio components it is advisable to consider the suspension system and the additional load requirements you are asking of the springs and shocks. This is another reason to start with high-quality, performance-engineered suspension components.

Since 1988, in-dash cassette players have been replaced with CD players, which in turn have given way to CD changers. As of late, in-car video cassette players have been upstaged by DVD players. By 2004, high-tech fully functional telematic programs will replace today's navigational systems. It's the Carousel of Progress in living motion.

Far and away the most significant progress has been made in under-the-hood bolt-on performance products. In 1988 the majority of small car enthusiasts knew where the hood release was located—and that was about the extent of their technical knowledge. After years of education and product development, sport compact car owners have become trendsetters in technology and are contributing to the cutting edge of modern automotive performance.

Some air systems are short pipes, supplying a greater volume of air to the throttle body. Others are true cold air intakes that grab cooler air from outside the engine compartment. A wide range of styles and colors are available.

The number-one under-hood performance item is the air induction system. Some are short pipes that allow for greater airflow and volume. Others are more advanced, featuring longer pipes that grab air outside the engine compartment, thus providing cooler air to the throttle body to create more potential horsepower. Superior engineered long-pipe systems are also designed to increase the velocity of airflow as well as air volume. Combining cooler air with greater quantity is the key to maximizing horsepower gains.

Headers can create additional horsepower depending on the application. Honda's factory Civic exhaust manifold (pre-2000) was very well engineered and required the aftermarket to perform extensive R&D to improve upon it. For other makes and models, the results are more favorable.

After air intakes, the next most popular change is plug wires. Of all the fancy wires that have come and gone, horsepower gains have been slim and hard to document. However, some wire products do help energy travel to the spark plugs in more efficient patterns, delivering small power gains and reduced emissions.

An exhaust header is often seen under the hood. These items can be both good and bad—even at the same time. For example, Honda spent millions of dollars to develop its exhaust manifolds. The result was that Honda Civics, Accords, and Preludes, as well as Acura Integras, were fitted with a stock part that out-performed 99 percent of aftermarket products while delivering better performance throughout the torque range. The one advantage to the aftermarket product is its lighter weight.

The same was found to be true on 1990–97 Mazda Miatas. An aftermarket header added about two horsepower. Second generation Miatas (especially 1999 and 2000), on the other

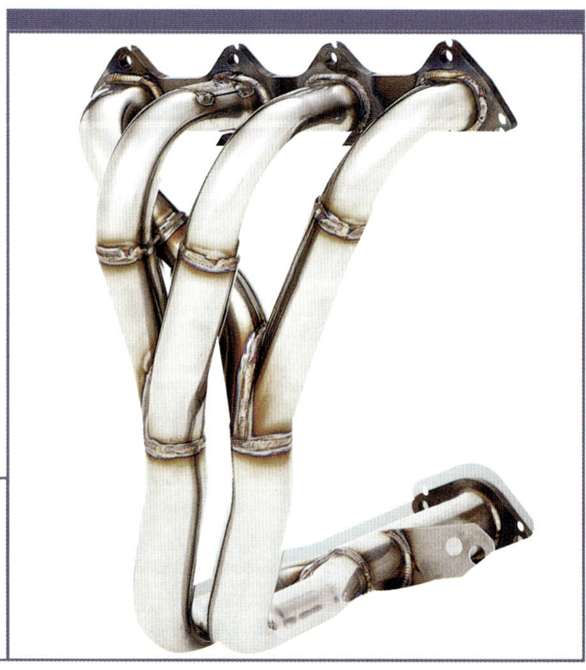

hand, benefited from an aftermarket header by as much as 12 horsepower over models fitted with a factory exhaust manifold and pre-cat.

A more potent and powerful modification is a performance exhaust system (from the cat-back). Exhaust systems are made to flow burned gasses in an efficient manner. Performance systems improve flow in proportion to the engine's ability to create power. Overkill is overwhelmingly evident in the sport compact arena, as three-inch-diameter systems are adapted to engines that could produce equal or more power with a two-and-one-half inch system. The primary reason to install a performance exhaust system is to improve the audible sportiness of the car (so it sounds more like a race car). This is not to say that a well-engineered exhaust system won't improve power—it will, as well as offer more immediate throttle response. It is the sound that makes the biggest impression on many car owners, and not the performance potential.

Moving into the creature comfort area of the car, the first item that is generally installed is a massive tachometer with a shift strobe light big enough to illuminate an entire city block. Necessary? Perhaps. Overkill? Definitely. Gauges are vital to monitor important engine functions and are fairly easy to install. Aftermarket companies have developed window pillar pods that provide room for boost and vacuum gauges for cars equipped with superchargers or turbochargers. The aforementioned shift lights can be helpful while racing

One of the easiest and most rewarding upgrades you can make (on most models) is a performance shifter. Short, precise shifts are essential to smooth performance driving. Usually only a few hours are required to swap out the factory banger with a better-engineered aftermarket unit.

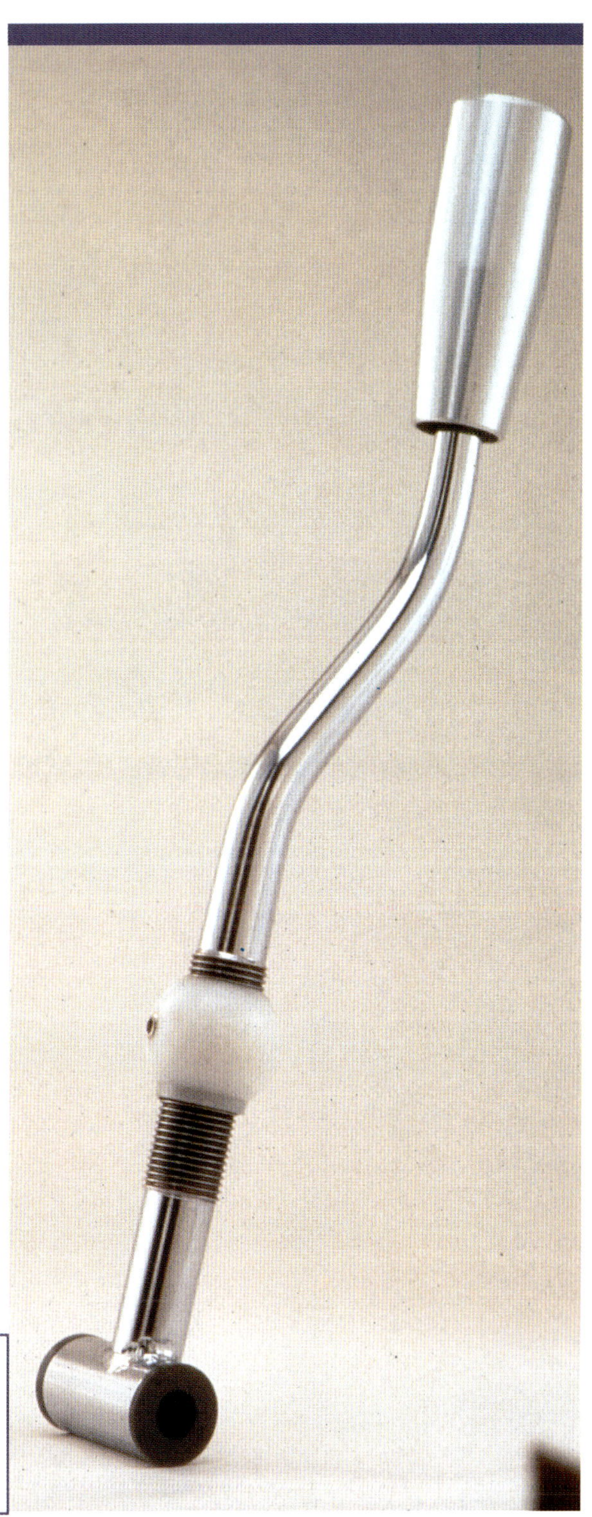

In the sport compact world anything goes. There are no borders to bump up against when the imagination is put into play. This Civic hatch features a well-executed plan of tasteful paint, styling enhancements, mesh grilles, chrome-plated wheels, and the right stance. *Lowrider Magazine*

to remind the driver when the engine's optimum up-shift rev points are reached: a good idea, especially when combined with a rev limiter to keep from spinning the engine into impending death. In other words, build a failsafe into the car and do not rely solely on the precision of the tach or shift light.

Those who race, or just want the seating stability of a racer, find harness belts and racing seats an interesting touch. Be aware that racing seats can get uncomfortable and are hard to get in and out of on a day-to-day driving basis. Racing seats do provide vastly improved biofeedback to the driver and promote performance through stability. Factory seats are designed to fit the masses with comfort and easy ingress and egress. Performance cars often feel as if they are sliding during demanding turns when it is actually the driver in the seat that is being pushed from side-to-side.

A popular fashion statement has been to gut the interior to give the appearance of a competition car. The original intention was to reduce weight, shedding non-essential items such as door panels, carpeting, consoles, rear seating, headliner, and even window glass (replaced with fixed Plexiglas). This is basic and cool, but should you gut your interior, save all

Making it go is one thing, getting it to stop is another. Braking systems can help you drive with more confidence and wait to brake even later before corners. Balancing the front and rear braking systems is the key to precise control. Simply jamming on huge front rotors and a multi-piston caliper is not the complete answer. Planning will save time, money, and bodywork.

Lightweight components, such as on this Civic, can serve a dual purpose–they shed weight and provide good ol' fashioned fresh air to the engine. Of course, in this case, the weight saved by discarding the factory steel hood was negated by the additional weight of the styling package and rear-deck wing.

the factory trim items. You may want to reinstall them at a later time.

One of the real charms of the sport compact hobby is its diversity. Different styles, attitudes, and building approaches have manifested themselves through the exterior of the cars. Here, anything goes—from wild paint to minimalist approaches like shaving and primer coating. Some car owners sport the beauty factor of finely trimmed styling packages to enhance the factory bodylines. Others elect to trim away the excess and project a beater attitude. One item that is universally accepted is a rear wing. Ironically, rear deck wings provide little usable function on front-wheel-drive cars. Wings were developed for rear-wheel-drive race cars to produce down-force, thus improving drive-wheel traction. Since most sport compact cars are front-wheel drive, the presence of a rear deck wing is more for show. Nevertheless, rear deck wings are a staple item in our world—and a little vanity is allowed.

Where body development has taken a sharp turn in the right direction is in the creation of lightweight components,

Supercharging supplies consistent, reliable power throughout the rpm range. While no piece of cake to install, most well-engineered kits can be installed over a weekend. Tuning doesn't require a master's degree to achieve desirable results.

such as hoods and trunk lids made from carbon fiber and fiberglass. These items can shed as much as 50 pounds of unneeded sheet metal, supports, and hinges. That type of weight loss can make a tremendous difference in a Civic, Miata, Eclipse, or Integra. Many aftermarket hoods are formed with air scoops or ducts to funnel rapidly moving cool air into (or hot air out of) the engine compartment. This makes these items dual-purpose—less weight, more performance.

Over the past decade huge strides have been made in improving braking. Where once small front discs and rear drum brakes were the norm, multi-piston calipers and cross-drilled and slotted rotors are prominent via easy bolt-on applications.

As with all modifications, balance is the key to total performance. It is a common error to over-build the front brakes—causing a severe nosedive under demanding situations. By creating proper proportioning between the front and rear brakes, slowing and panic stopping can be achieved with ideal balance.

A good braking system will allow you to hold your straightaway speed longer before entering a turn during autocross and track events. On the street, you can feel greater ease in slowing and improve your driving confidence under all conditions—wet, dry, heavy traffic, winding roads, and on either asphalt or concrete surfaces.

When discussing modifications, there is no better way to finish than with the big three: superchargers, turbochargers, and nitrous oxide. These are the heavyweights of bolt-on products. Each will produce dramatic horsepower gains, each will require more extensive installation time and talent, and each will set the bank account back several thousand dollars. In the same vein, each will require you to upgrade your driving skills.

There has been an ongoing debate over which is better supercharging or turbocharging. The answer is "yes." Both forms of forced induction will provide high levels of performance. The differences between the two are many, and there are many benefits.

Superchargers provide smooth, consistent power at low boost (between six and nine pounds). For example: a supercharged 2000 Miata with a 1.8 liter engine (140 factory horsepower) will dyno in the neighborhood of 224 horsepower at the wheels. Similar results are easily achieved with the 1999 Honda Civic Si and 2002 Focus SVT. The earlier Civic Si jumped from 170 to 235, and the Focus SVT went from 180 to 242 (using the Jackson Racing system).

Supercharger installation is generally straightforward, requiring anywhere from eight to 16 hours, depending on application and experience. The long-term durability of a supercharger is generally very good, and added engine strain is minimal.

Turbocharging can provide massive horsepower gains—enough to push your back flat to the seat. One of the major differences between a supercharger and a turbocharger is that the turbo uses spent exhaust gases to spin the compressor. Superchargers, on the other

There are three types of superchargers: Roots, twin-screw and centrifugal. Each performs the same basic function in slightly different methods. This Vortex unit (on a Civic Si) increased horsepower to nearly 300, providing a wild ride during the first few test drives.

Turbo units like the one on this Miata can be upgraded to a greater extent over superchargers. The downside is that turbos usually require additional and on-going tuning. This system requires 26 hours of labor to install. The performance was breathtaking, as peak rear-wheel horsepower jumped from 112 to 187 at just seven pounds of boost.

hand, require the crank to drive the compressor. Turbos take some time to build boost, providing a feeling of normal acceleration and then suddenly rocketing to warp speed. This requires more driver talent both when racing and on the street.

Turbo installation is a far greater test of mechanical skill—taking even experienced gearheads as long as 25 hours to complete (before tuning). The rewards of the extra effort are more potential and versatile performance.

Turbos can put greater stress on internal engine components than superchargers—changing the long-term service life of the engine. To reach its potential, a turbo system should include an intercooler—a system that routes the compressed air from the turbo unit to a compact radiator cooled by air that flows over its fins as the car moves forward.

The cost of superchargers and turbochargers is somewhat comparable. Be aware that not all forced-induction systems are CARB or EPA approved and may require some fancy footwork prior to state mandatory emissions testing and certifying.

Nitrous oxide (often referred to as NOS—short for nitrous oxide system) provides power through a chemical reaction that supercools the air/fuel vapor, allowing for more vapor to be compressed in the combustion chamber. The result is a more violent combustion when the spark ignites the vapor. The piston is more rapidly driven down, creating more power to the crank. This is a simplified definition of how nitrous works.

Used properly, nitrous can be the great equalizer between larger-cubic-inch V-8 engines and compact inline four-cylinder engines. In many cases nitrous can add 50 percent more power in short spurts.

There is a price to be paid for this magic gas. Nothing will destroy an engine faster than an overshot of nitrous. Often called "go juice" or "running on the bottle" (nitrous oxide is housed and dispensed from a pressurized tank that looks like a scuba tank), improperly introduced nitrous can cause the air/fuel mixture to lean out. Uncontrolled detonation within the engine's combustion chambers can explode with such force that pistons blow apart, connecting rods bend, or the crank snaps. All these events happen on a regular basis.

The easy way to avoid any of this damage and still gain the performance benefit of nitrous is by using a regulator that monitors the air/fuel/nitrous mixture and can automatically stop the flow of nitrous before lean-out occurs.

Bang for the buck, nothing adds horsepower like nitrous. Just be informed that nothing can be more damaging to an engine than the misuse of nitrous. The rule to remember before pushing the flow button is all things in moderation.

THINGS TO REMEMBER:

- Lower is not better.
- Louder is not better.
- Power does not always equal performance.
- Performance without driver talent means nothing.
- 1,320 feet equals 1/4 mile.
- Autocrossing is fun . . . . lots of fun.
- There's a difference between quick and fast.
- Show and go can live together in harmony.
- You always get what you pay for.

There's magic hidden in a bottle of nitrous. The engine go-juice supplies instant speed by super-cooling the air/fuel mixture, allowing the cylinder to pack in a greater amount of explosive molecules. When used correctly, nitrous can get you there (the finish line) in a hurry. Used in the wrong fashion, a tow truck will be your ride home.

A dead give-away that a turbocharged monster is breathing down your tailpipe is the grinning innercooler mounted front and center. Air is forced through the fins, cooling the turbo's compressed mixture before it enters the throttle body.

CHAPTER 6

The past five chapters have provided insight into the history and the cars that make sport compacting what it was, what it is, and perhaps what it will become. However, without the enthusiasts, all we have is sheet metal, alloy, and rubber.

Who we are, what we are, and what we do are the essence of our sport. If you listen to the marketing experts, everyone with a tricked-out import car is between 17 and 28 years old, lives in California, drives a slammed Honda with 18-inch chromed wheels with an exhaust tip of the same size. We have 3.5 tattoos, multiple piercings, and listen to boomin' hip-hop and techno music from 1,000-watt audio systems while street racing on moonlit business park pavement.

Okay, that's how they see us. But, who and what are we, really? The answer is as diverse as the style of personalization we perform. True, a majority of sport compact car enthusiasts are under 30 years old. True, California is a primary gathering point and can be identified as the birthplace of the sport. The facts are that the age spread is from pre-driver's age to well into the 40s and 50s.

As for geographical limitations, there are none. Sport compact car involvement spread in

The Sport Compact segment transcends ethic and gender lines, reaching a large number of enthusiasts. A large majority of participants did not grow up in a car culture family, creating a new generation of performance and custom car enthusiasts.

Unlike other automotive groups, sport compacting knows no geographical boundaries. Shows, such as this one in Georgia, attract vehicles from surrounding states.

a fashion unlike that of hot rodding, mini-trucking, and muscle cars. While all of these auto interests can be traced back to the sun and sand of SoCal, sport compacting exploded onto an entire nation, at the same time.

Over the first decade (1988–98) participation at events grew from a handful of cars and 100 spectators, to full-blown spectacles with 5,000 cars on display and 50,000 spectators. At these events the diversity becomes apparent, but what is also evident is that no one seems to notice or care. It is one mammoth family of car enthusiasts.

The media has helped the sport grow at an unprecedented. When *Sport Compact Car* first appeared in December 1989, it was the only

▼ SPORT COMPACT MAGAZINES COME AND GO

Sport Compact Car	*Honda Tuning*
Turbo	*Miata Magazine*
Super Street	*Velocity*
TMR	*Tuning Concepts*
HCI	*510 AGAIN*
Max Power	*Car Craft*
EuroTuner	*Lowrider Euro*
Import Racer	*Street Power*
Street Racer	*Street Legal*
Import Tuner	*Performance*
Import Racer	*RPM*
Grassroots Motorsports	*Street Customs*

friend of the industry on the newsstand. Since that time, more than 20 titles have joined the cause. Some passed away in a quiet whimper, while others grew to become a force in the automotive print world.

The Internet has been a boon to the sport. Because the two interests grew at the same time, many sport compact car enthusiasts were also into cutting-edge computer technology. It seemed that everyone with a Honda and a computer had a web site. This is not to say that all the information was credible or accurate, but it was accessible.

Eighty-five percent of sport compact car enthusiasts are under 30, and 81 percent are male. While the vast majority is male, sport compacting has the largest percent of female participants of all automotive interests (19 percent). The two largest ownership blocks drive Hondas (35 percent) and Acuras (9 percent). Of the Hondas, 21 percent are Civics and 9 percent are Accord models.

Vehicle popularity is where some differences between Eastern and Western owners begin to surface. Honda, Acura, and Toyota are the big three out West. In the East, Honda has the top spot, but Ford products skip over Acura and Toyota to be the number two choice – albeit a distant second. On the lower end of the scale, the Dodge Neon has less than one-half of a percent of the Western attention, but is about 1.5 percent of the Eastern scene.

To show how important style and image are, more than 64 percent of enthusiasts polled by leading magazines listed appearance or exterior styling as the number one reason for their buying selection. As for driving purposes, 85 percent use their cars as daily transportation.

What all the surveys and focus group studies show is the high level of energy and enthusiasm behind sport compacting, not just

as a hobby, but as a lifestyle. Our cars are at the center of nearly all activities. On a daily basis, our cars help us get involved with car clubs, friends, family, weekend plans, weekday activities, where we drive, who we drive, where we park (usually away from other cars to eliminate possible door dings), and why we seek out others with similar interests. We completely immerse ourselves, heart and soul, into the culture. It is a passion driven by speed and beauty. Some call us sport compacters, import racers, tuners, speed freaks, import geeks, and ricers. It—matter doesn't—we're in it for the duration.

Over the past decade, education has taken the sport to escalating heights. Much like the hot rodders of the 1950s and street machine crowd of the 1960s and 1970s, the sport

While performance is at the heart of the sport, 64 percent of enthusiasts list appearance as the number one notivation in a make/model buying decision. *Mazda*

compact car generation has spawned a new form of gearhead. While it is unlikely most can rebuild a Holley 780 double-pumper carburetor, many can plug in a laptop computer and alter the fuel flow or ignition timing to optimize performance for 1/8- or 1/4-mile runs.

Of all the uncalculated data, what is most important is the number of owners who gather together. Clubs are an important focal point.

Results from industry studies reveal a unique trend. A disproportionate number of sport compact enthusiasts were not exposed to custom or performance cars as a family activity or interest during childhood. An entirely new chain for future generations has begun. The same studies show that of the primary age group (18-32) who were part of a household where a father or uncle was into hot rods or muscle cars retained an interest in traditional V-8, rear-wheel drive domestic cars. What this says is the current trendsetters are forging new roads for generations to come.

Events are just part of our social interaction with one another. Sport compact car enthusiasts are a new breed, and take little lead from hot rodders and muscle car owners of past generations.

carParts.com
www.speedopt___.com
TOYO TIRES

Street, strip, sport, and show are the dominant venues that motivate enthusiasts to design and build their cars. Each has its own allure, rewards, and hazards. Each makes demands and requires compromise. All command dedication to achieve a high level of recognition.

Street Scene

Far and away, the largest sport compact car stage belongs to the street. This is the foundation for participation because its requirements are basic—a car, a valid operator's license, a working knowledge of the road, and a place to see and be seen.

Main street cruisers and boulevard marauders are the artists of the street—a canvas painted with light dancing off polished and chrome-plated wheels, exhaust notes echoing off of buildings, and the sweet reflections of hammered-down compacts in storefront windows.The street scene is a diverse affair and brings together enthusiasts who gravitate to varying styles. City streets, urban interstates, and rural highways are the arteries that connect to the heart that is the sport compact population.

Action takes place on both sides of sunset. During the day, an impromptu display of vehicles in the daily commute turns into an unscheduled parade down the interstate. Or it

The number of pro-built compacts has created its own league of big-time drag racing teams and drivers. Some high roller teams are approaching the six-second barrier.

The street is the primary playground for the vast majority of sport compacters. Doubling as a daily driver as well as a symbol of self-expression, building a car that thrills the soul and comforts the bank account is an achievable goal.

The camaraderie of turning wrenches and automotive discovery has expanded the sport's cohesive community. Whether its a weekend project or pulling all-nighters to get ready for a race or show, sport compact car enthusiasts are remarkably team oriented.

might be a show or club outing that brings a healthy gathering of enthusiasts together.

While the nighttime scene is all about glamour, the weekend and late night garage action provides a gritty balance within the sports. The wrench turning and the innovations necessary to improve performance have created a new age of hot rodders reminiscent of the generation that popularized automotive customizing in the 1950s.

A speed mentality binds together this cross-section of society. There is camaraderie among the sport compact community that glues veterans and newbies together in a mentoring process. Adding to the cohesiveness is a melding of talents and creative thinking. The garage is where this comes together.

As vital as the city scene is, the street can also be a dangerous and deadly place to play.

On-track racing is a growing sport, but street racing is a mounting problem. Many cities have created unique laws to slow down the rapid growth of illegal drag racing.

Street racing has reached epidemic proportions in cities across the country. As spectator and participant numbers grow, so does vehicle damage, driver casualties, and deaths attributed to illegal drag racing.

Southern California has always been a hotbed for street racing. In the late 1950s, throughout the 1960s, and into the 1970s, the police chased the problem, but put little coordinated effort to stop what was then a nuisance. Street racing, like all vehicle performance, took a break in the late 1970s to the mid-1990s. Then, as sport compact car enthusiasts looked for venues to test their driving skills, street racing returned with a ferocity not seen since the early 1960s. Street racing has become such

For many sport compacters this is a favorite sight – the Tree. In front 1,320 feet of acceleration. Behind, the other car.

Import drag racing has exploded from small tracks to major venues such as Englishtown, New Jersey, and Pomona, California. Participation has skyrocketed as well to make, compact car drag racing the fastest–growing sport in America.

a health and safety issue that many cities and counties are banding together to create special task force units to eliminate illegal drag racing altogether. Some cities, such as San Diego, California, have created legal street racing areas where racing is controlled and monitored, with timing equipment, classes, and prizes.

Strip Scene

On a nationwide basis, legal and organized drag racing has become one of the most popular forms of motorsport. The sport that traditionally catered to domestic muscle cars and specially-built cars powered by American V-8 engines seemed like the last form of racing that would appeal to far lesserpowered inline four-cylinder-equipped compact cars. However, Frank Choi had a vision in 1990 that would create a home for enthusiasts shunned by drag racing promoters and track managers. Choi worked on a grassroots movement to create the first "Battle of the Imports" event at Los Angeles County Raceway in the desert township of Palmdale, California. The turnout was modest, but the enthusiasm was overwhelming.

Before long, the first Battle spawned a second, then a third. Participation doubled and tripled at each event. Spectator count grew to numbers too large for potential sponsors to ignore. Import drag racing spread like wildfire across the country. By 1998, five major organizations or sanctioning bodies promoted compact car drag racing.

As the sport grew, so did the sophistication of the cars being driven. The first sub-eight second run in a front-wheel drive car happened on May 14, 2000. Eight seconds was the import drag racing's version of the four-minute mile. Once it was proven that eight seconds could be broken, it didn't take long for a host of teams to topple the once formidable barrier.

Continued growth has brought in the sport a separation between novice and professional racing. By 2002 the sport was divided into the haves and have nots and created an opportunity for other forms of motorsports to attract an escalating number of enthusiasts looking for an avenue of speed status. This, in its own way, also contributed to the growth of street racing.

The sport now has its own league of professional teams and drivers that are well funded by sponsorship dollars. Television coverage, celebrity status for the drivers, and massive brand awareness for sponsors has also occurred because of the sport's popularity.

Sport Scene

The roots of compact car motorsports can be found at autocross and on-track racing events. These venues take cars and drivers up-hill and down, and require left and right turns, acceleration, and braking, and fuel and tire management.

Autocross is for everyone who wants to experience the thrill of racing at an economical cost. Cars at all levels of modification and drivers of any skill level can compete. The cars race against the clock on a closed course marked by traffic cones.

Import drag racing's league of professional drivers has grown to a point where the more successful enjoy celebrity status. Here Stephan Papadakis, driver of the AEM Racing Civic, signs autographs during a recent International Auto Salon.

Autocross is grassroots motorsports at its core. The only requirements to start racing are a car that will pass a basic safety inspection, a helmet, and a small entry fee. Just one day at an autocross event can provide a wealth of driver feedback. Novice drivers quickly find that they bump up against the walls of their driving talent long before they find the true limits of their cars' capabilities.

Before you head for the autocross, put together a few basis items: a jack, jackstands, basic tools (including a tire gauge), drinking water, a helmet, folding chair, light snacks (such as energy bars), a few quarts of oil, an extra set of spark plugs, a few extra ignition wires, jumper cables, and a canopy for shade (if there is room). These items will help you before and after your runs.

Autocross events are an excellent way to build driving talent and hone techniques, such as finding the apex of a corner and turn-in and power-out points. These events are loads of fun and can become addictive.

The next step up from autocross is actual fender-to-fender on-track racing. This requires much more skill sharpened talents, and nerve. You'll also need a bigger bank account because track cars are generally purpose-built and not streetable. However, a growing number of automotive enthusiasts are taking advantage of open-track days at their local road courses where street cars can be driven to their limits at higher speeds available through autocross.

Show Scene

Car shows have always been, and will always be, the primary activity for all things automotive. This is where ego allowed to run amuck. From small club shows to massive national events, show time is primetime.

For a short time, America had its version of the European Touring Car race series. This spawned a new interest in road racing and road racing wannabes. The styling carried over onto street cars and sparked some owners to try SCCA-style autocross events.

Low-cost racing does exist in series such as Spec Miata. With limited modifications and specific rules, a Spec Miata can be built for under $10,000. It's a lot of fun for low bucks.

Showing off your sport compact is an activity that can be progressive, and requires as little as extensive detailing, to ridiculous amounts of chrome plating and thousands of dollars in custom paint. The pace and investment is up to each car owner to determine.

The magic key to building a show car is planning. Putting together a blueprint for

Shows, from small gatherings to mega events, are the focal point for many club activities.

Show cars can be subtle, Euro-styled, and monochromatic, or over-the-top and outrageous. The level of modification and investment is up to individual taste and financial capabilities.

success will help save hundreds, if not thousands, of dollars. A plan will help avoid modifications that are later reversed or discarded. This also goes for parts and accessories that will be swapped out for something else later.

Some owners prefer to leave their cars factory-equipped, especially if it has some level of collectable status, such as a first year Acura Integra Type R. Others find nothing sacred and can't wait to add personal touches to the most exotic cars.

There is a wide range of show classes that range from showroom stock to radical custom.

Competition-style cars can also find a home at shows. Whether it street competition or a car in full race trim with is cage and scraped paint, the show scene is a place to see everyone's individual automotive dreams.

Club Scene

Whether an owner's interest lies in street, strip, sport, or show, clubs are where all sport compact car enthusiasts come together to share experiences. Clubs, from small local or regional groups, to national organizations with thousands of members, provide cohesion to the sport.

Before joining a club, check out its reputation. Contacting a car club council in the area can be a big help. Ask what the club's standing is, if there is any. Another excellent contact is your local police agency. This sounds a bit odd, but think about it: if the club is on the outs with the local crew in blue, you may be getting into something that will put a clamper on your enjoyment. If the club is involved in community projects and has made a stand against illegal street activity, involvement could be even more rewarding.

If a club doesn't exist in your area, or you and your friends want to start your own club, ask yourself what you want out of a club. Is the purpose to race, show, or just hang out with a group of other car owners who share the same passion for sport compacts?

First, develop club bylaws and reasons for joining. These items accomplish a number of things, but most importantly it will bring your club respect and attract the type of owners you want to be associated with. If you set up your club in a proper fashion, it will quickly grow.

The most important factor in running a club is inclusion. Never judge a potential member by the quality of their car. Membership quality is far more important than how many trophies a car wins or how fast it is on the track.

Choose your members wisely and act responsibly. Banding together will greatly strengthen the sport. Well-run, solid clubs provide a greater acceleration to the sport and enhance the enjoyment of owning and building a sport compact.

Events—street, strip, show or sport—are designed to showcase the creativity of the craft and bring enthusiasts together under the common bond of performance, no matter how the word is described.

CHAPTER 8

What does the near and distant future hold for sport compact car enthusiasts? No one has a crystal ball, but there are clear signs that point to continued growth. One of the most obvious indications that sport compact cars have become part of the general performance automotive world is the reaction of big car manufacturers. A look at what is happening with racing's most prestigious sanctioning bodies also validates the solid foundation of the sport.

Car makers from Detroit to Japan have gotten into the tuner business. This is evident because there are many factory hot rods and concept cars are being built and shown as the possible next generation of performance offerings.

In organized racing, successful events such as Battle of the Imports and the National Import Racing Association (NIRA), and Import Drag Racing Circuit (IDRC) have made the National Hot Rod Association (NHRA) stand up and take notice. Compact car classes are now a big part of the NHRA's future.

SCCA continues to develop programs to bring new participants into the fold. There is already a number of growing on-track classes, including a Spec Miata class that drew so many

The Maxima brought speed and style to Nissan's line of cars. This tuner version features an aftermarket turbo system to boost horsepower to 330. The ground-hugging suspension provides a smooth ride for the luxo-speedster.

The future of import drag racing is bright as the NHRA and other sanctioning bodies are acting upon something that grassroots racers have known since 1991—import racing can be big business and good fun. The popularity of drag racing now depends on small-engine platforms.

entries in 2002 that many races held qualifying sessions a day before the actual event. The National Association of Stock Car Auto Racing (NASCAR) has even come around. The once exclusively domestic sanctioning body is now involved with Toyota to bring import branding to its major series' races.

The car show circuit is already extensive and reaches from coast-to-coast, will only get bigger. The growth of events such as NOPI (Georgia), Carlisle (Pennsylvania), and Hot Import Daze/Nights (California) has proved large venues can be filled. These shows have already recorded spectator counts from 35,000 to 94,000. Those numbers are close to Super Bowl-type numbers, and there is no end in sight.

The people in high places are listening, taking notes, and making business decisions based on what we, as sport compact car enthusiasts, are doing and saying. This is the future of the automotive market, we own it. It's no longer all about cubic inches and smoking rear tires. Sport compacting has changed the way the auto world thinks.

If one idea has been planted in the minds of auto designers, engineers, and executives, it is the demand for more speed, style, and sophistication. This idea is pushing them to new heights, we are demanding more. The automotive aftermarket has also stepped up its efforts and will continue to help push the edge of the envelope. Compact enthusiasts want more and express the attitude, "Either help us get there, or get out of the way and feel the wind as we pass you by."

Perhaps the whole idea of creating high-performance cars from econo-boxes wasn't

There was a time when the future of compact cars meant small, boxy, boring sedans. Because of the enormous popularity in sport compacts, manufacturers now have a completely different view of the next generation of cars. *Ford Motor Company*

born in America, but we have accelerated the process like a dragster on nitrous. Sure, this happened in Europe and Japan decades ago, but the American sport compact car movement, with its enthusiastic southern California roots, has made it more than a worldwide trend—it is now an established part of the car culture. Sport compacting has created an entirely new generation of hot rodders who helped revitalize the entire performance and custom car community worldwide.

Manufacturers are becoming tuners, this Ford FR200. In a *Motor Trend* track test, the 304 horsepower, turbocharged pavement burner ran head-to-head with a Corvette Z06. Ford has made many of the FR200's components available through its Performance Parts division.

INDEX